WOMANISTCARE:
HOW TO TEND THE SOULS OF WOMEN
Volume 1

Table of Contents

Table of Contents cont'd

DEDICATIONS

To Chuck; my life's partner and friend
To Eleanor Miller; my counselor and prayer warrior
To Valerie; my Poet Laurete and Sister
To Daisy; my "Sisthur" who loves me
To Harlene; my right arm and support
To Greg, Grelon, Grian and Giraurd; all my children
To all my Sisters who push me to "write the vision
and make it plain"
To Woman To Woman Ministries, Inc; my hope for
every tomorrow
To God; my Creator and my Source

Linda H. Hollies

WOMANISTCARE

Preface:

It's a new day! It's a new time! And, this volume is a new view of pastoral care which focuses on the tending, sheparding, nurturing and specific needs of African-American women. In this age of womanist wisdom, philosophy and theology a group of seminary trained, professionally prepared, and clinically oriented and ordained pastors have collaborated in this work. What is new for this venture is that each contributor is African-American and female.

It's past time for us to speak for ourselves. Others have spoken to and for us; studied, analyzed and prepared documents about us; they have critiqued, criticized and been extremely critical of us. So we have decided to write our own story, tell our own tale, record our own history and leave our own truth in print. This volume in no way presupposes to be the "complete" word about the experiences and needs of African-American women. It's only our first volume!

We write for our sisters who care. Each writer is a caring sister who has academically prepared to assist the people of God to move toward wholeness and full potential development. However, because each writer is of the female gender, our care and ministry flows out of our womanist understanding and experiences of God. We know how often our needs have gone unmet, our tears have been unseen and our cries dismissed as "silly". It is because we want no other sister to experience this painful neglect that we write.

As African-American women who are professional pastors and care givers it is our mandate and burden to share what we have learned on our journey. For too long we have searched the shelves, perused the syllabus, combed the books and listened with our spirits, hoping to see ourselves in the textbooks of theological education. We are living proof that we exist. Our bloodlines and family ties prove that women of color have been on the scene of history. Yet, we are painfully and oftimes, deliberately absent from the literature. To correct decades of academic silence, we have gathered to write.

An interdenominational sisterhood, we are United Methodist, Baptist, Independent, African Methodist Episcopal and Church of God. We are senior pastors, associates, clinical pastoral education supervisors, chaplains, employee assistance reps and ecumenical consultants. We are married, single, mothers, divorced, middle thirties to middle fifties in range. We are short and fat, tall and thin, colorful and plain, introvert and extrovert in make-up. Our unity lies in our commitment to God, our people, the sisterhood and dedication to the education of the people of God.

In July of 1991, we gathered as sisters at Michigan State University, Lansing, with a group of African-American women at Woman To Woman Ministries "Advance". An intergenerational group we were randomly mixed in small groups for a weekend. Each contributor led a small group who brought personal issues of care and concern, as well as baggage and garbage collected through the years. Much of our writing has been informed by this significant sharing experience. It is with great anticipation that we await the unfolding of our next "Advance" with God!

This book is dedicated to the Sisters of Woman To Woman Ministries, Inc. We owe a special debt of appreciation to the Lansing Chapter who hosted us and made possible our space and format for the birth of this venture. Without their labors of love, this infant would not have been born. To the significant others in our life who blessed us with nurturing resources, encouragement and listening ears, we dedicate this first volume of our love and care. To God be the Glory! And, we've only just begun.

Linda H. Hollies

Meet The Contributors

Marsha Foster Boyd is Instructor of Pastoral Care and Counseling at United Theological Seminary in Dayton, Ohio. She is an ordained elder in the African Methodist Episcopal Church and serves on the General Board of The Christian Church (Disciples of Christ) and is a member of The American Association of Pastoral Counselors. Marsha has written several articles and conducted numerous workshops and training sessions. She is completing PhD requirements at Graduate Theological Union and received her M. Div. from Interdenominational Theological Center in Atlanta, Georgia. She is married to Kenneth Boyd and the mother of one daughter, Evette.

Delois Brown-Daniels, M. Div., Yale School of Divinity, currently heads the Clinical Pastoral Education Program at Northwestern Hospital, Chicago, Illinois. An ordained American Baptist Pastor, she is Associate on the staff of Trinity United Church of Christ in Chicago. A reknown preacher and teacher, she has conducted numerous seminars, workshops and retreats, as well as run revivals and stirred hearts as Woman Day Speaker across the country. Delois is a certified supervisor in the American Association of Clinical Pastoral Educators and a fellow in the

College of Chaplains. She is married to Dr. David Daniels and mother of one son, David, Jr.

Janette Chandler-Kotey, M. Div., Oral Roberts University, currently serves as Senior Pastor of the St. Lukes United Methodist Church in Tulsa, Oklahoma. Completing degree requirements for a Doctorate of Ministries, Janette serves as preacher, praise leader and workshop leader for numerous women's gatherings. An ordained elder in the United Methodist Church, she is married to Raymond Kotey and mother of Lillian NaaDei (Queen), Rita Kouko (Second Daughter), Jennifer Kochoo (Third Daughter).

Roberta Collins, M. Div., The Chicago Theological Seminary, has spent the last seven years of her life as Chaplain at St. Bernards Hosptial in Chicago, Illinois. Ordained in the Baptist Church, she pastors the Christ Center of Truth, Chicago, Illinois, which she founded. An organizer of womens retreats, Roberta hosts several institutes each year which features education, training and motivation through speakers, workshops and seminars. Married to Robert Collins, she is the mother of Justus LaDarrell and grandmother of DeJuana and DaShauna.

Valerie J. Bridgeman Davis, M. Div., Austin Presbyterian Theological Seminary, serves as one of two clergy couples who co-pastor the

Banah Full Community Church in Austin, Texas. Ordained by the Church of God, Anderson, Indiana, she has served as writer for their Shining Light Survey, a denominational magazine as well as writer for Pathways To God, a church devotional and Sunday school materials. Valerie is a much sought after workshop and seminar leader who brings much to enrich our lives with her poetry and reflective writings. Presently, she works as Communications Coordinator for Austin Metropolitan Ministries, an Interfaith Group, and continues her clinical pastoral education ties through her work at Seton Medical Center in Austin. Married to Rev. Don Davis, she is mother to Deon and Darus.

Jerri E. Bender Harrison, M. Div., Garrett-Evangelical Theological Seminary, Evanston, Illinois, is currently enrolled in their Doctorate of Ministry Program, Pastoral Counseling track. An ordained elder in the African Methodist Episcopal Church, she is assistant pastor to her husband the Rev. Peyton Harrison at the Wayman AME Church in Chicago. A renown preacher, Jerri ministers to all persons, and yet has a special ministry and care for women. Both a writer and musician, Jerri is mother to their son, Brandon and expecting her second child.

Linda H. Hollies, M. Div., Garrett-Evangelical Theological Seminary, Evanston, Illinois, is senior pastor of the Richards Street United Methodist Church in Joliet, Illinois. An ordained elder in her denomination, she spent two years as a resident and supervisor in training in Clinical Pastoral Education at the Catherine McAuley Health Center in Ann Arbor, Michigan. Author of *Inner Healing for Broken Vessels, Restoring Wounded Warriors and Womanist Rumblings*, she has contributed to several books and numerous magazines. Married to Charles H. Hollies, she is mother to sons, Greg and Grelon, and daughter, Grian. She is grandmother to Giraurd Chase.

Eleanor L. Miller, M. Div, Garrett-Evangelical Theological Seminary, Evanston, Illinois, is currently employed as Employee Assistance Manager at the Mercy Hospital and Medical Center in Chicago, Illinois. For many years she worked as In-patient Clinical Coordinator for the hospital's substance abuse treatment center. Active in recovery and prevention circles, Eleanor teaches, lectures, serves as a resource person and does many seminars. An ordained Baptist minister, she currently serves as assistant to the pastor at Mount Zion Baptist Church in Evanston, Illinois.

Gale Kennebrew Moore, M. Div., Chicago Theological Seminary, met a committee this year for certification as Associate Supervisor in the Association for Clinical Pastoral Educators. She presently serves as Staff Chaplain at the South

Chicago Community Hospital in Chicago, Illinois, and is a fellow in the College of Chaplains. An ordained Baptist pastor, Gale preachers, does workshops, seminars and small groups. She is the mother of three children, Michael, Angela and Matthew.

Mary M. Wise, ACSW, and M. Div., The Chicago Theological Seminary is pastor of South Deering-Pullman United Methodist Churches in Chicago, Illinois. Mary has an extensive background in both the clinical social work field and pastoral experiences. Ordained in the Northern Illinois Conference of the United Methodist Church, Mary does preaching, teaching, workshops and seminars which pull together the multi functions of ministering to the whole person. A writer, poet, consultant, Mary is mother to son, Daniel and daughter, Carmieka.

A Letter From Our Technical Editor:
Yvette Avery-Irizarry

I have been tremendously encouraged on a personal level by reading and working with the contributors of this volume. As an active and born-again Christian, who teaches high school English, this has been an extension of my ministry to our God. For I see *WomanistCare: How to Tend the Souls of Women,* as a challenge from God to all women in the world today. God is looking for women that are willing to take a stand and rise from their places of lethargy and slumber; women who are confident in their own faith and self worth. God continues seeking women who will embrace forgiveness and employ their God given gifts to the fullest. This type of woman is both incredible and victorious! This volume challenges each woman to stretch out on her faith and do as the anonymous author of this poem suggests:

Doubt sees the obstacles. Faith sees the way.
Doubt sees the darkest night. Faith sees the day.
Doubt dreads to take a step.
Faith soars on high.
Doubt questions, "Who believes?"
Faith answers, "I".

This poem captures the popular song we sing, "Here am I, Lord, send me." This book will challenge you to "GO"!

Through the redeeming nature of our Savior, these writers have overcome many of life's encompassing circumstances and accepted Gods divine strength as their anchor. They rejoice victoriously over what the world may perceive as hopeless or impossible and offer spiritual remedies so that the suffering common to all women can be seen in the light of the Holy Spirit. Isaiah 42:3, states "A bruised reed shall not break..." and this truth echoes on each page of this volume.

This books accepts no compromise for the women of God. It challenges maximum potential for those called to ministry. This work is direct and pungent. This work allows each of us to move from silence and acceptance into love and appreciation for our fullness as woman. Included is a chapter for every woman, whether lay or clergy. Some of you will read this text and immediately rejoice. Others of you will recognize harsh realities and become further challenged. Each of you will hear loudly the call, "Go ye, therefore, and teach... Teaching them to observe all things...and lo, I am with you always even unto the end..." (Matthew 28.19-20)

I praise God for African-American women/sisters who did not allow the fear of writing to prevent us from sharing and profiting from their experiences and education. Their determination to tell these stories has allowed me to utilize my gifts and skills to make this a "gift of love" to the world.

I pray that you are blessed in your reading and application of their theories. It is my sincere hope that you will accept your mission and go forth!

Do You Have Time To Listen
I Have a Story To Tell

Sit, please, if you will.
Pray, do you have time to listen?
Busy? Yes, I know, sister. So am I.
But the story inside has beat down my silence and
 demanded a voice.
I have one now: But voice without audience means
 NOTHING.
And nothing has been my meat way too long.
Eat with me from the table of my secrets.
Drink from the well of my longings.
It is a gift I ask of you. Listen s l o w l y and
 pardon me when I pause.
Know the story is Rewriting while I tell it.
Sister, do you have time? I have some serious story
 to tell.
Will you listen?

                    Valerie J. Bridgeman Davis
                       October 23, 1991

INTRODUCTION
Linda H. Hollies

WOMANISTCARE:
CARING THROUGH STORYTELLING

With great fanfare and creativity the producer had the set built to specifications of striking proportions. Nothing like it had ever been seen before! Those who were to play minor parts and supporting roles were brought on board. The script called for two major characters, whose parts would greatly influence the overall production. They had to be the most perfect specimens of their time--the high excitement, thrilling drama and magnificent set would overshadow them if they were not superbly matched to carry off their roles. The two were hand picked to dominate the center stage with enough energy that the others could simply respond to their lead.

After a stunning publicity campaign had been orchestrated, the names of the two leading characters were released. Adam and Eve, let your story begin! So starts THE STORY of God's interactions with the world. The drama began in the Garden and has been continually unfolding, changing plots and twists everyday since. The characters change but THE STORY remains basically the same.

The first book of the Christian Bible, Genesis, means "the beginning." And it starts with the words, "In the beginning". The activities of the Creator are detailed for our knowledge, our education and our appreciation of the world in which we live. Moses, another character whose life has touched ours, compiled and wrote THE STORY of our ancient past. Being male, he told it from his world view. We have a powerful male producer, God, a powerful male villain, the serpent, and a powerful, but gullible leading man, Adam. The one whose story has never been told is Eve. Others have told her story, but always from their vantage point in history. Adam was the first one who pointed the finger of blame at her and her story has been a twisted plot and evil tale since. Yet, Eve had her own story!

A story relates our personal and individual history. A story ties us to the Universal plot of life and other characters. A story is an invitation for you to connect with others whose life is similar and yet unlike your own. A story reveals the drama, the tragic, the wonderful, the comedy, the horrible and the awesomeness of your existence. All stories do not have "happy ever after" endings. This only occurs in slap-stick comedies. There must be challenges, questions, pain, mystery and searching for a story to be authentic. A story reveals what has been worth noticing and keeping track of in your life. All stories need both a teller and a listener. There has to be someone who will record the events and someone who will lend an "open" ear and receive the details without judgement, censorship or criticism. For stories are a gift to be shared. Eve had her own story! Who listened and who cared?

This is the essential "beginning" when caring for women, learn to listen as you appreciate and affirm them telling their own story. Every woman has a story to tell. Her story is unique, particular and important to her further development. Telling her story will allow her to make sense out of what has "felt" like nonsense. For in telling her story she will begin to make the connections between what has already happened and what is occurring in the present. In having someone listen to her story, receiving it as a gift that is shared, her value as a human being is appreciated, raised and admired. This simple act of active listening will enhance her sense of self-worth and raise her self-esteem.

I sat in my office, visiting with one of the local physicians. I became aware of voices being raised in the secretarial complex. I tried to ignore them, and raised my voice to keep the doctor from hearing the increasing confusion. All at once the situation escalated and there was no denial of its presence. There was this explosive outburst and the sound of violent hammering and stumping. As I bolted from my office, I saw a woman beating on the counter with both hands, tears were streaming down her face as she screamed at one of the male employees, "I am not crazy! Get out here! I am not crazy!" The man just stood, looking at her, silent.

As I asked him to leave us alone, I gently placed my hand on her shoulder and enquired, "Sister, what is wrong?" She began to calm down, but the tears continued to flow. I waited, just holding onto her hand, my visitor forgotten. When the rage inside settled enough for her to speak, her few words explained all of the violence she had exhibited.

4

She looked at me and said, "Nobody ever listens to me!" No other words were necessary. I felt her pain. I was quite familiar with her story.

Storytelling is the gift of self-disclosure. When someone dares to listen with openness and comprehension, the teller can take off her mask of hiding. Women have been forced to lie, to build defenses and to "act" in certain ways because no one wanted to listen to their "real and honest" story. "Everybody" already "knew" the STORY of EVE! Why listen to a repeat of a familiar story? Yet, Eve never got the opportunity to tell her own story!

"In the beginning" connects all of us with the Creator God. This is the ultimate connection in each of our lives. All of our stories are tied to this "beginning". Power for living is generated when this realization strikes us where we live. When you are the listener to a woman's story, often it becomes your privilege to remind her of this fact. She needs to be made freshly aware that she is not alone; that there is a grand purpose for her life and that her role in God's story is of great value. This is your gift of appreciation given to the storyteller.

Your life is tied to the storyteller! For THE STORY is older than our recorded history. God has a story that precedes the Moses story. Your storyline is involved with that of your sisters whose is tied to that of Eve who is a direct connection to God who has no respect of persons and created our Mother Eve with sensitivity, care, love, power, intelligence and dominion. The planning of the grand design of Eve predates that of the Moses story! And Eve has not

5

told her story!

Stories are not limited to the powerful survivors of the worlds history. The weak, the insignificant and the victims have their story too. Every nation and race of people have their own set of stories which details the heroes and seldom the heroines. For stories fulfill our basic curiosity about the past, our origins and our beginnings. Stories help us to utilize our imagination to "see" from where we have emerged. Stories entertain. Stories keep our customs, values, beliefs, hopes and dreams alive. Women of every culture have a story to tell. But, Eve has not told her story!

For as many individuals who have lived upon the face of the Universe, there are that many stories. Everybody has a story. Each of us begin and end and have plots and storylines that unfurl in the middle. Drama, comedy, mystery and complex issues make for a good story and these limits play themselves out in the lives of everyday women. A good suspense novel, a "who-done-it", holds our attention. A good and exciting love story grips our hearts and a real life Erma Bombeck makes us laugh at life's funny presentations. Stories are the vehicles for carrying forth the continuation of our connected lives. We live on in the stories told about us. But, if we don't learn to tell our own story, how much truth will be told? Remember Eve's story!

It took me 43 years to find a group of individuals I could trust with my story. My outward cover looked fine, my presentation to the world was "in place." Yet, my story was a "text of terror", with much pain, hurt and shame involved. Being a survivor of incest by my own father was "the" secret I had kept to myself for all of my life. I had never heard anyone tell a story of this nature. Surely, it had only happened to me and I must have been the blame.

In the summer of my first year of seminary, I took a quarter of Clinical Pastoral Education (CPE). I was one of six students and we had a female supervisor. On a hot summer day, I was to share my family history. I decided to risk telling them my story. I narrated it from a second party stance, very removed and clinical in nature. When I finished, there was silence in the room. I sat, looking around at each of them, waiting for some response. Finally, the youngest woman in the group, who we had named "Baby Sister" in our family system, spoke up. She looked me in the eyes and said, "Linda, that's a very sad story and I feel like crying. You don't always have to be strong, you can cry about your pain." The tears came. My healing began.

"There are eight million stories in the naked city. And, this is just one of them!" So, began the telling of a long-running television drama told from the perspective of city police. Yet, the important thing to remember is that the "crooks" had a story to tell from another view point. As women enter your office and need to tell their story, you will be reminded of your own story. Good and effective pastoral care says that you must put telling your story aside! This is not your time or your place! You are the receiver of the story, the listener with an "open"

7

ear. The telling of your own story must be done in ways and with others who appreciate a good story. As the pastoral care provider, at that particular time, your story is not the most important.

Too often the listener becomes the storyteller! Even the giving of helpful hints and pertinent information is not necessary for good pastoral care. Listen, receive, acknowledge and affirm as Eve pours out her heart and shares the details that make her who she has become. Question her for clarification. Press her for connections between tales. Look her in the eyes with interest and compassion and let her tell you her story. Laugh with her, cry with her and do not offer her pity!

Evil touched Eve's life and she was forced to make a decision. Choices continue to present themselves to each of us, often times in the crisis periods of our lives. Pity does not force us to make good and quality choices. Pity will allow us to continue on the path of destruction. On the other hand, empathy assists women in affirming that, "Yes, evil is here. It is a fact of life. And what choice will I make in this instance?" As an empathetic listener, you can help Eve see both the lessons she has learned and the blessing she has received even in the midst of being touched by evil. Stories teach us about living life in more productive and growthful ways.

Working with a colleague who was in both pain and denial, I decided to try and "reach" her with the sharing of my own painful story and the struggle I was involved in while seeking for wholeness. We sat in her office and I was open and honest about my childhood trauma. She looked at me and cold, unfeeling and unhelpful to my process toward inner healing. Her own untold pain prevented her from being able to affirm my pain. Later, I was able to share with her my anger at her lack of response.

Your affirmation of Eve's story is many times the only rope she has to hang onto for survival. When you make brief connections into her story about the evil that has touched your life, you let her know that she is not alone, different or so bad until it's only happening in her life. "Yes, I've been there." "I personally have experienced that too." "That sounds like my story." These are the connectors which will encourage Eve to continue unfurling her untold storyline with you.

An effective and appropriate place for the sharing of your story is in the context of the sermon. The African-American community looks forward to the telling of The Story on Sunday morning. What is most often missing in the telling is the points which make The Story of old relevant and useful to the listeners today. Once again, the connecting threads could come from incidents in your life. The techniques of weaving the old and the contemporary require much prayer and much practice. You do not want to leave people with simply the details of your life, however, exciting or thrilling. You want to leave them with the hope found in THE STORY which became new in your life and can be made real in theirs. Ending this type of message with an altar call places the focus on the Rock of the Ages. To affirm, "*This is My Story*" prepares souls to be fertile soil for seeds of hope!

Evangelism is the arm of the church which reaches out to others with THE GOOD NEWS. In the middle of the word, evangelism, is the word, angel, one who brings messages of hope, help, healing and wholeness. Even when Eve's story has been filled with the terrible and the tragic, she should be able to hear a good word from the old story! The message ought to empower, destroy the yokes which have kept her bound in her "text of horror" and provide her with the knowledge that evil does not have the final word in her life. Any telling of the story which does not point to liberation, freedom and hope has been misinterpreted.

In the preaching arena, it is proper, correct and essential that you, as care giver, provide methods for practical application of the story's truths. Especially in preaching, you must build the bridge from the theology of the text to the life of the NOW for the listeners. Too many folk know about Daniel and the lions den, but they are not provided with instructions and details on how to operate in their own den. They can recite the tale of the Hebrew boys in the fiery furnace, but don't know how to deal with their own fiery furnace on a day to day basis! People need to hear stories which touch them where they live today. People need to know that they are not alone and that their story is not unique unto themself. People need to hear that God yet writes "good" endings to stories which sound like theirs.

In Africa there have always been storytellers. There were the resident and the traveling storytellers.

The resident of the village usually belongs to the tribal leaders family and had the responsibility of keeping alive the legend, myths, heroic tales and personal exploits of the tribe. The traveling storyteller went from village to village with tales, antidotes and folklore and told and collected other oral narratives to share. It is from this ancient tradition that much of our heritage and customs have been preserved. The storyteller was the historian who took the listener back to the days of "common roots". With the oral tradition, the storyteller evoked a sense of wonder, mystery and awe among those who listened, captured and shared "THE STORY". The oral tradition always pointed to the God who cared and was in control of the people of God. This God always had a "hero and heroine" to use for liberation and escape. This God came to America in the collective consciousness of every African and has been passed down to us.

The stories that we hear and the stories that we choose to tell allow individuals to know much about us, our values, our hopes and our dreams. We take something which we have heard, embellish it, add our personality to it and make it our "truth" which we want and need to tell. For storytelling is a creative art which can teach, give examples and clarify issues for both ourself and our audience. Stories "must" be told. The universal truth passed on in many stories belongs to no one individual nation or tradition. Universal truth belongs to all of us. There is something to learn in every telling, regardless to the adaptation for different cultural understanding.

Eve needs both to tell her story and to hear THE STORY which can transport her from her present reality into a place where she might encounter the mystical, mysterious and wondrous which is beyond her immediate grasp. Stories transmit images, ideas, motives, and emotions which she finds difficult to articulate. For a good story will express a "common truth" which Eve can comprehend and bring back to her reality.

A good storyteller is a creative artist. For in your telling of the story, you will add that which has influenced, taught and made your life better. Seldom will you tell the same story the same way. For the telling is impacted by your emotions and by the receptivity of your audience. Their interest will stimulate you, motivate you and "help" you to get your point across. Artist "feed" off of the energy that is around them. Your presentation will be greatly impacted by those who listen.

Stories change with the times. The universal truth remains the same. However, we try to conform the story to the needs and conditions of the day in which we live. Storytelling is a living art which preserves the past but becomes understandable in the "now!" It is your responsibility to make the "green pastures" relevant to those who live in urban and concrete jungles. It is your responsibility to make the Jesus of Jerusalem walk in the city streets, touching, listening and caring for Eve where she lives.

The real reason you tell Eve a story is to share with her. The real reason she will come and tell you her story is because she "feels" that she can share with you. Stories paint pictures of the way we view the world and how we make sense out of our life. Stories point beyond our immediate world to that world which is bigger than life. Eve needs to know that you understand and affirm her world. This is the manner in which we can present ourself to each other in "safe ways". Storytelling is a safe manner in which you and Eve can reach each other about your worlds.

Stories entertain, present knowledge, teach morals and values, pass on traditions and cultural heritages. Jesus was a master storyteller. The parables were always "right on time". They seemed simple and were easy to understand. Yet, there was always a deeper significance to the story than first met the ear. The parables were teaching tools which were effective. They were preserved, passed down, collected, retold and finally written in order that their "truth" might find us.

There were no televisions to entertain our African ancestors. The people of Jesus' day had no radio, newspaper or popular magazine. Most of these were farm types, hard workers who had little time or tolerance for "fun and games." Yet, each of these two groups utilized the power of story. For stories show the emotions of fear, love, anger, hate and passion which is basic to all people. Stories have the ability to answer the "questions" we dare not ask. In a story we can challenge the norms and social dictates of our time and location. We can enlarge our vision, our world and open avenues of exploration for others in the telling of a story.

Stories have the power and ability to sway our opinions, to convince us and to empower us to dream. There is magic in stories. The wonder of "once upon a time" magically transports us to another world and another time. New insights and revelations emerge in the sharing of story. For "new" truth is unveiled as we listen to those in a different time and another place. We are connected to the universal when we engage in storytelling. For all of our stories are intertwined with God's!

Eve must tell her story! She wants to be in relationship to other human creatures. She wants to be acknowledged as one who counts, one who has contributed and one who matters in the larger story. Eve needs to belong. She needs to understand how she fits into the world. Eve needs to know that God loves her in spite of the stories that have been told about her.

Can you even begin to imagine the joy, excitement and awe that Eve experienced "In the beginning...?" When she was proclaimed "good and very good", when she saw the love, wonder and joy of the man, Adam who welcomed her as equal partner, what were her feelings and thoughts? As she viewed the majestic, the grand and the spectacular, can you hear her words, see her smile and feel her sheer delight?

As you sit in your place, in your time, you can get a glimpse of her first day. Her story begins to unfurl itself in your mind! Eve was there when it all began. She has her "version" of THE STORY! She will tell you "her story" if you will sit and listen.

Without a listener, there can be no story, for there is no one to receive this gift of love and wonder. You help her to tell her story in the mutual give and take of storytelling. Her story will bind the two of you together in ways that questions and answers and surveys cannot. Statistics and research data are not the flesh and blood who was affected by life, reacted to life, endured life and has an authentic story to relate.

Eve will be your guide to discoveries of "her world" even as she re-visits her past and sees it from a different perspective. She needs to "unmask the mysterious" reasons for her story having been buried and unheard for all of these years. Eve's story is the "missing piece" in Scripture. Named "the Mother of all living things", she has had direct impact upon the life force of the ages. She is often left unnamed, called, woman, daughter, wife, or even "a certain woman", but seldom has she been called by name or allowed to speak for herself.

How would Eve tell her story? Listen carefully to the stories of the women you encounter. Encourage them to return to "the beginning", and let THE STORY unfold!

Bibliography

Cassady, Marsh *Storytelling Step by Step*, California Resource: Publications, 1990.

Bausch, William *Storytelling, Imagination and Faith*, Connecticut: 1989, Twenty-Third Publications Mystic.

Williams, Michael, *The Storyteller's Companion To The Bible*: 1990, Abington Press.

William, White *Stories For The Journey*, Minneapolis: 1988, Publishing Company.

Thulin, Richard, *The "I" Of The Sermon*, Augsburg-Fortress, 1989.

Jabusch, Willard, *The Person In The Pulpit: Preaching As Caring*, Abington, 1980.

Smith, Christine, *Weaving The Sermon*, Westminister Press, 1989.

Glaz, Maxine & Moessner, *Woman In Travail and Transition*, Jeanne Fortress, 1991.

Proctor, Samuel, *Preaching About Crisis In The Community*, Westminister Press, 1988.

Hicks, Beecher, *Preaching Through A Storm*, Zondervan Press, 1987.

Those Preaching Women, Mitchell, Ella Pearson, Judson Press, 1985.

Forbes, James, *The Holy Spirit and Preaching*, Abington, 1989.

Patricia Bell-Scott, et al, *Double Stitch: Black Women Write About Mothers and Daughters* Boston: Beacon Press, 1991.

Linda Gass and Marian E. Barnes, *Talk That Talk*, New York: Simon and Schuster, 1989.

Hold Your Voice There, Mister

Hold your voice there, mister:
      I can speak for myself!
      Yeah, you used to talkin' for me
            like I'm mute or deaf or plain
not here --
But
      I got somethin' to say and,
      since you never been inside my
Soul,
      you just list'n awhile.
            I dream my walk
                  everyday,
      and sometimes declare
            this just the way it is --
I'm not backin' up or flinchin'
One inch.
      Seems everytime I pause,
      You open your mouth ready to explain
      away my potential --
But,
      I can speak for myself, and,
      since you never been inside my
Visions,
      you just pay attention.

Valerie J. Bridgeman Davis
April 27, 1991

CHAPTER 1

The Challenge of WomanistCare
Eleanor L. Miller

Jasmine admired the arrival of summer as she flew to Middlesex, Pennsylvania. She and Daisy had known each other since that first women's conference when it seems as though the second chapter of Acts had been revisited! Something had happened with those women until they all felt it must be continued. As these two women were reunited annually for this spiritual Advance, their bond seemed to strengthen. As hard times have a way of pulling families closer together, their sisterhood was woven last year as though their two mothers were the same person. It would take a miracle for the scripture to be true in this situation, Daisy had often thought, "All things work together for the good of them that love the Lord; for them that are called according to God's purpose." Daisy had rehearsed this scripture in her mind, sometimes even doubting, in her singleness, whether or not she really loved the Lord because she was certain that the Bible was right.

Well God had blessed, the Bible was in fact true, and Daisy had gotten married. Jasmine had been in the wedding, and Daisy gave her no choice about coming to celebrate her husband, Nelson's, birthday. They considered it something of a rebirth, as this was the first time they had celebrated as a couple. The unsuspecting Nelson picked Jasmine up from the airport, glad that she could stop by for a visit while she was on the East Coast. With the wisdom that only a virtuous woman possesses, Daisy had successfully pulled off the surprise party not only under Nelson's nose, but also with his help. She had made sure everything was perfect. He was king of their home everyday, but he could have been mistaken for a Tutankhamen this particular day, the way family and friends fussed over him.

The morning after floated in with rain and Jasmine raced to beat the sun up, which by the way never showed. She insisted on fixing breakfast for everyone before anyone could argue with her about it. In ones, twos and threes, the house guest woke to the smell of scrambled eggs, snowflake rolls, grits, bacon, sausage, coffee, and freshly squeezed orange juice. Daisy wanted to scold Jasmine for cooking for such a large crowd single handedly, but her words were drowned in the aroma of the food. The room was only large enough to accommodate half of the group, but the living room easily converted into an extended dining room. There was much laughter as they exchanged comments between the kitchen, and dining room about the events from the previous evening and the plans for the day.

It was Sunday, so the food was eaten quickly with morning worship service in mind. Plates were scraped, glasses were drained, and folks scurried about the house trying to get dressed in times. Competition was stiff for the two bathrooms, one iron, and bedroom mirrors, but in short order everyone was dressed and ready for the short drive to Beacher Avenue Church of God. The pastor wasn't missed as the Holy Spirit seemed to speak through anyone willing to stand behind the pulpit. Associate Pastor Hardy preached until the power of God fell. It was like the grand finale to the party that had started the night before--God was praised, God's Word was celebrated, and the people rejoiced. In a smorgasbord of praise, laughter and conversation, Nelson led their guests back home to the "tornado" they had left the house in that morning. The crowd had left without the Mrs., as she found dreary weather reflected the exact sentiments of her physical condition.

Ignoring the protests, Jasmine dutifully marched to the kitchen to pick up where she had left off. LaChelle, an older relative of Nelson, joined her. Jasmine actual welcomed her help deciding that more would be accomplished if the two of them worked together. LaChelle began running dishwater as Jasmine put away the left over food. "What are you doing with those grits?" LaChelle asked as she saw Jasmine pick up the pot, walk toward the garbage, then turn back standing in the middle of the floor staring at the grits in the pot. The butter had left a yellow film on top, they were cold, crusted and separated from the sides of the pot. Still Jasmine just stared. LaChelle walked over, assured by this time that Jasmine had seen something crawling in the post. Jasmine finally spoke. "I don't know, but I'm not going to throw them away." "Why not?" LaChelle questioned, "Who's going to eat left-over grits?" LaChelle was clueless as to Jasmine's mental whereabouts; for in Jasmine's mind, the grits had already been transformed into something else--she had just not figured out what that "something else" was yet.

Soon the grits became as clay that a potter had partially used and was now preparing to begin a new project with the remains. She just couldn't throw them away. She felt compelled to make something out of them. It was a though she remembered the mess that her life once was. It had been very appealing at one time, all things beginning in order. Then somewhere, somehow, things just changed. Nothing seemed right. She didn't really remember how much time this change had required--hours, months, years, whatever. There had just been a time in her life when she was like left-over grits: used up, unwanted, detached...Someone wanted to throw her away.

Old friends, paramours, employers, family, herself--it wasn't clear exactly who, but somebody wanted her to just disappear. And perhaps for a short time she did. But then, this Potter came along and looked at her. The Potter smiled, then began recreating her. Scraping off the yellow crusted dross that left a film over her life, then adding a pinch of this, a dash of that and....

In *In Search Of Our Mother's Gardens*, Alice Walker defines a Womanist. The woman who is "outrageous, audacious, courageous and willful in behavior: is simply womanist. She is a feminist of color; one who seeks to know more than what is good for one; one who seeks to be responsible, serious and in charge; one who enjoys woman's culture, and women and men sexually or nonsexual. She is a universalist that embraces all of life." A womanist is a soul. A womanist needs soul care.

Soul care has traditionally been the functional responsibility of the pastoral minister. It is that function whereby the minister attends to the inner life of their parishioners. Soul care is a developmental process through which we do special things in cooperation with God through the life given us in the new birth (Lord, 1990).

Pastoral ministers must be certain about the nature of their vocation. It would be misleading for a pastoral minister to respond to the ministry of soul care as if it were equivalent to the care provided by social workers, physicians or teachers (Ogden, 1983:187). Pastoral care is unique in that it holds an inherently greater weight than other professional relationships because it deals not only with the body and mind, but with the soul--the eternal existence of humankind (Ogden, 1983:187).

The soul is that which animates the body and causes it to deeply feel, to know and to will (Ogden, 1983:186). Audrey Lorde describes the erotic in terms similar to theological definitions of the soul.

Further, the erotic is the nursemaid of our deepest knowledge; the connecting source to ourselves which causes us to feel and express the sensual (Lorde, 1984:56).

There are four identified functions of the ministry of care: healing, sustaining, guiding, and reconciliation. Healing restores people to wholeness by helping them overcome impairments. Sustaining helps people endure and transcend a circumstance which seems impossible or improbable. In guiding, we assist people in making choices, making them aware of alternatives. Reconciliation seeks to reestablish broken relationships (Clinebell, 1966).

Womanistcare incorporates these key elements into a model which focuses on the long neglected needs of African-American women. Needs of being restored, needs of being loved, needs of being validated, needs of being acknowledged, needs of being respected--the list is endless. The most effective pastoral minister is aware that the very nature of their role carries with it tremendous responsibility in that she is accountable for the care of a person's soul, which is a serious eternal matter. When we examine the intricacies involved in the soul care of women such as these, we come to understand what an awesome responsibility lies before us. How do we begin to care for those whose existence has been nearly invisible to society and whose personhood has been unesteemed and unapplauded? The faces of such women have not been seen, their voices have not been heard and, their desires, dreams, hopes and aspirations have gone without validation. Do we dare attempt to provide care for a people who through history, tradition, culture and religion have been an illusive entity devoid of feelings and thought? We must. We must care for these women, for they are our sisters. They are our very selves.

It is therefore imperative that we construct a facsimile which represents women as they are today as a result of societal influences. It is within the context of my years of clinical experience in chemical dependency and pastoral ministry as an African-American woman that I reflect.

Biblically, the perception of women is comparable to that of property. We are considered as something to be owned or possessed. We are regarded as subhuman, having no rights or privileges, unlike our male counterparts. We are debased, devalued and considered socially inferior. Scriptural interpretations are the albatross around our necks as we have been told by those in authority that our lives are to be worked and lived out through the pleasure and beckoning call of men. Images of a woman seeking to discover her identity are squelched as we are taught religiously to be the scriptural Marthas, diligently working for others at the expense and abandonments of ourselves. African-American women are neglected and kept in subjugated positions of the church even though they are the major contributors to the spiritual development of its parishioners and the financial security of its parish.

It has been appropriately stated that the African-American female has been the bond that maintained the community. Despite the dehumanization of women through scripture and their lack of powerful positions, history records the vigilance of a few Black women who had the nerve and the courage to dare to make changes within and without our churches and our community. Of significant notation was the institution of Women's Day--an event which uses one Sunday to focus on uplifting the gifts and talents of women (Ruether, Keller, 1986:121). This dream of a Baptist woman, Nannie H. Burroughs, has impacted all of the major Black denominations for there are annual Women's Days across the country.

We live in a patriarchal society which continues to use scripture as a basis for societal structure. As Black women we encounter a triple edge sword which locks us into a self-perpetuating system of racist, sexist, and classiest oppression. We have struggled on the periphery of this white male dominated society trying to gain access to participation as equal human beings. The difficulty of reaching this goal persists because academia has used the sciences and arts to support their claim that we are an inferior people.

Culturally, we have been socialized into the belief that we are second class citizens who are unable to think or feel on our own. We are a people who, even in the face of expressing an opinion or thought, have been denied the privilege of naming our own reality. We are socialized to develop a sense of "femininity" by identifying with our mothers. Our nurturing traits instruct us to show concern for the comfort of others. We are attuned to the needs of others to the complete abandonment of our own comforts. The Song of Solomon states that we tend to the vineyard of others and allow our own vineyards to go to waste. We have an insatiable way of making ourselves indispensable to everyone, including our children, husbands, lovers, parents, relatives and friends. We have given to the point of making ourselves ill, suffering ailments of various physical complaints because we lack the skills to say "no". We have learned that in our culture, sickness is our only legitimate way of receiving temporary sanctuary from the demands of life that we have been taught are ours and ours alone to endure.

Our psychological expectation, to fulfill our emotional need to be needed, often causes us to be enmeshed in the lives of others to the total disregard of self. As a result, many of use are, in contemporary language, suffering from co-dependency. Co-dependent women fail to realize that soul care is due them. Women whose lives have been affected by alcoholism, drugs, physical and verbal abuse are blind to the fact that they deserve care. They are so ensnared, anxious, confused and fearful that they remain in relationships where they are battered and bruised because they aren't aware that there are options available which can assist them in getting out of crippling situations. Our lack of confidence to believe that we can survive independently handicaps and can harness us into roles as impotent, docile women. Our misplaced values for materialistic gains interferes with our ability to pursue a sense of self.

The acculturation of African-American women within the white male dominated, capitalistic society has been the expensive price we have paid to fulfill our need to belong. These values are so intrinsically internalized that in the face of self endangerment we remain faithful to a value system that is destructive to our well being. Our creative gifts and talents have not been widely celebrated as they have been banished to the side and slighted as insignificant.

For too long we have walked in the shadows of America's high premium value on skin color and the effect upon us has been that of poor self esteem and self worth. And yet, with all the raising of consciousness about our blackness as a thing of beauty to be embraced, today women are still agonizing over the pain and suffering from their experience of skin color. All too often we have not participated in celebrating our heroines.

We stand on the shoulders of women like Mary Bethune, Sojourner Truth, Harriet Tubman, Nannie Burroughs, and Ollie Laurence, who in mid-life decided to return to school to learn how to read and write, not to work toward a diploma or GED, but for her own self enjoyment. We weren't taught their stories which spoke of their strides and struggles for liberation. So we are without understanding of who we are as African-American women. Given the conditions, conventional and feminist models of counseling have inadequately addressed the care needs of women of color. In short, they have been irrelevant.

The conventional counseling models of care are Eurocentric and operate from a male bias, excluding women's experience. In practice, this model has worked with distorted information and is therefore invalidated by the authentic study of developmental psychology. Developmental psychology clearly teaches that the make up of woman is different than that of man either through nature or nurture, and that the whole process of self is different for a woman

(Gilligan, 1982).

Conventional models are weak in consideration of gender issues and have neglected to reflect upon or even consider the rich cultural background of women. Traditional models uphold the value system of the Western world that esteem the pursuit of independence and individual gains. In our quest for independence we isolate ourselves from others, making it easy for us to be impersonal and detached from our humanness. Consequently, these models create a gulf that separates one from God's plan for us to be relational and live within community.

These approaches are therefore ineffective in terms of the pastoral care function of guidance. It is the minister's responsibility to offer advice regarding choices and alternatives in the assistance of care. This approach is ineffective in presenting to women a powerful influential role as a desired option in dealing with inner conflicts. The conservative counselor usually offers options which sustain women in a submission, subservient role that is restrictive and unfulfilling. Maintenance in a prescribed role is of minimal help and counter productive to the primary goal of counseling, which is to move a person towards self actualization.

I have encountered women who through the counseling of a conventional ministry approach resulted in some damaging affects to her psyche because of a limited world view by the minister. This very lopsided counseling perspective gave rise to the need for an approach which serves to liberate women; hence we have the feminist perspective.

The feminist approach derived its impetus from the women's movement in the 1960's. A movement which was helpful in that it heightened the consciousness of women regarding their right of choice. It emphasized that women could elect to work or be a homemaker. The feminist approach stresses the idea that care of women must be rethought to include gender issues of women. The feminist are most highly critiqued for their assertion of women as universal, being from the same Eurocentric perspective as their male counterparts without any consideration of women of color or women across cultures. The feminist approach is a limited resource because it presupposes that its experience speaks for the diversity of women when in reality it only serves the overall needs of white women, leading to another oppressive structure for African-American women. The divided agenda of feminists leave people of color on the periphery. It is contended that the key issue for white women is the rise of inclusive language and female imagery.

African-American women's needs are centered on more expedient issues such as equal salary for comparable work. The feminist agenda is therefore largely irrelevant to Black women's issues because we are at different points on Maslow's hierarchy of needs.

Feminism assumes a hostility between African-American women and men because it is pro-separatism. This separatist attitude negates the reconciling function of the pastoral minister which is to facilitate wholeness through forgiveness. The issues among African-Americans are too crucial for us to adopt a separatist view point, we must work together. The relationship between African-American women and men is in dire need of healing. It is imperative for us to understand that our quarrel is not amongst each other because we are mutually oppressed and fighting many of the same battles. A separatist position would be detrimental to the African-American community. We need to confront all of the problems within our community, and work together toward common goals.

As we reflect upon the impediments and barriers to the healing and caring of the souls of African-American women through the critique of conventional and feminist methodologies, is necessary to argue the challenge from a womanist perspective of helping Black women develop into their inherent potential.

The pastoral minister embraces a model of care that tends to deal with issues of concerns from a deficit model of defining and addressing problems, often guided by the willful behavior of the minister. We should rather do therapy from an asset model, which accentuates the positive within the client. Emphasizing our assets affirms the belief in women's culture and love for women, and most importantly acknowledges women's experience as a source from which to do ministry.

Doing ministry from a womanist approach forces African-American men and women to wrestle with their issues with one another, contrary to a feminist approach of separatism that would keep us alienated in different corners enhancing the scapegoating of each other, which society perpetuates. For we have believed the societal assertion that the perils of the Black man are perpetrated by the Black woman.

Womanistcare proposes that as women are taught to recapture the value of communal and familial life, diminishing the focus on individualism, the quality of our lives could be enhanced because we would be promoting a concern in relationships over the value of materialistic gain. How do we parent the process of guiding women towards their potential? We have reviewed the definition of a womanist which states that she is one who enjoys the culture of women. To appreciate one's culture is to have a sense of pride and respect for one's people, which directly increases self esteem. At this crossroad we can learn from Lorde who well articulates the necessity of African-American women to be educated and literate because they are the imperatives to moving us into more effective roles. As long as we are illiterate, uninformed and uneducated we have no power to reach our potential. This potential is rooted in our acting responsible enough to walk in the belief that we have choices. Knowledge of our choices informs us that we contribute to the decision making process which includes the mastery of how to take care of ourselves.

...Jasmine realized that as the Potter had made her over, she had been given the right to care for herself. In absence of a caregiver--that is some one who gave a care about the leftovers of her life after she had been spent to the benefit of others--she had something within that could nurture her back to wholeness.

Suddenly she knew. "Grits pudding!"

"What?" LaChelle exclaimed.

"Have you ever had grits pudding?" she asked LaChelle.

"Had 'em," LaChelle responded, "I've never heard of 'em".

"Me either, but that didn't stop God from making human beings", she laughed. "No, think about it." Jasmine was serious again. "They make tapioca pudding and rice pudding, why not a grits pudding?" Jasmine began moving fiercely around the kitchen gathering ingredients. Immediately those countless hours spent as a spectator in her grandmother's kitchen paid off. She turned on the oven, emptied the grits into a larger bowl, then broke the congealed pieces with a big spoon. She added pineapple cream cheese spread, vanilla extract, whipped eggs, sugar, butter, milk, half and half, cinnamon nutmeg, and crushed walnuts. After stirring all the ingredients together, she poured the mixture into a baking dish, topped it with two leftover crumbled rolls, and placed it into the oven. Shortly, the aroma drew curious noses into the kitchen from all over the house. But the inventors would not reveal the contents of the oven, leaving the anticipators in sweet suspense.

Soon it was ready. Jasmine pulled it out of the oven as they smiled realizing the great feat they had accomplished. It was through grits pudding that

Jasmine understood the revelation of what the Potter had done with what had been the remains of her wasted life.

"But Jasmine, who is going to eat something called grits pudding, especially when they know we had grits left over from breakfast?" LaChelle wondered aloud.

She paused and thought about the scars, the wretchedness, and the gloom her life once was. She remembered being leftover and almost giving in to thoughts of allowing herself to be permanently thrown away. Then the Potter stepped in, wiped away the dross and made her into the person that people know her to be today. But God not only recreated her, God also put the power of recreation into her hands...."and when you are converted and made new, strengthen and establish others". The scars of experience made her see the leftover grits not for what they were, but for what they could become. Now that they had become something new, the old things were passed away; same essence, different substance. "Anyone who experiences our creation won't realize it was made of leftovers," Jasmine retorted cleverly.

"Hey wait a minute. That's it. We can call it Creation." LaChelle suggested.

Jasmine had quickly grabbed a spoon and moved to taste the pudding. She then stated triumphantly, "As God said, it is good."

African-American women have served in similar capacities as grits. Just as grits are a basic food source for most African-American families,

Black women have been foundational in maintaining the stability of our community, as well as the American community at large. Grits are a primary source of grain, providing iron for the body. We also, by the products of our spirits, minds and bodies, have fed those who have come in contact with us, providing vital nourishment and nurture for them. We have often been referred to as the "mule for which all society rides". As inexpensive as grits, our labor has historically been a mass productive, highly marketable, overused, undervalued commodity. In slavery we kept alive both our families and their enemies, who each ate from our hands and drank from our breast. Like the grits we have been left replete. We remain at the mercy of someone who will realize that even after being used by many, we yet possess the same nutritional value, and with a little care, we can once again be desirable. With our begged, borrowed and stolen labor, we have been the primary care givers for a society who has dictated to us that it is our daily obligation to provide care. As did those grits, we long to be discovered by Jasmines who will realize that we have more than one use and that we are multi-purposed.

To be respected and treated with dignity are elements of the pastoral relationship. Jasmine's attitude regarding the grits was that even though they were cold, hard and crusty they were salvageable. They were worth using all of her abilities and instincts to facilitate their transformation. Jasmine's deliberation over whether to save or discard the grits points to how easy it can be for us to thwart our creative flow.

We often do this either through our lack of sensitivity to how our lives are connected to God's unfolding drama, or our refusal to believe that God's works amidst the mundane are no less miraculous than those amidst the spectacular.

LaChelle and Jasmine cooperated with each other during the creative process, allowing an opportunity for mutual bonding. They utilized their limited resources of time, energy and re-creative experience by pooling together. In this relationship they became a two fold cord that could not be easily broken.

Pastoral ministers can help facilitate bonding or a sense of belonging by encouraging collaborative groups to network. Historically, African-American women usually formed a strong safety net for protection through activities like quilting, canning, cooking, sharing recipes, caring and visiting the sick.

What would our lives be like if more people were encouragers like LaChelle? LaChelle's role of midwife helped Jasmine birth the pudding into reality. Affirmation and validation were the ingredients used by LaChelle while assisting Jasmine with the pain of decision making. LaChelle offered Jasmine a listening ear, a helping hand, a supportive will, and encouraged her to take a risk. She validated Jasmine as a human being with the right to dream and to envision, to think and to feel, and to express the erotic or creative within. This is an inspiring example of sisters participating in creation together, each respecting the role of the other.

The selection of the ingredients highlights the importance of spontaneity in the creative process that directs us towards wholeness. Somewhere a willingness should emerge to be open to the insights within.

Sharing with one person at first and then, step by step, as with the adding of ingredients, we can open ourselves to others, creating an avenue for them to receive from the process. The real excitement arises when we recognize that our being courageous enough to deal with the restlessness of creative movement touches us in splendid ways, and allows others to benefit from our gifts.

Tending to the souls of women means that through proper exegetical work, we teach women how to be fully alive and fully aware human beings. It means that we love them enough to say that the consciousness raising of the sixties is insufficient to meet the demands and issues of the nineties and beyond. The sixties era served its purpose to make us aware but it is now time to make movements towards complete wholeness. We need to empower women by educating them to the rhythm of life that has deep roots, that connects us with our ancestors who have historically been adaptable and flexible people, who have survived because of these qualities. We need stories in our lives which transcend from the oppressive circumstances that seek to entrap and ensnare us. It means that we love them enough to work beside them, fight for them, and stand with them. It means that iron sharpens iron as we, as individuals, glean from the collective, yet diverse fountain of wisdom, experience and life which is the Black woman. The challenge of womanistcare pushes us to look at the creative force within each of us that liberates us to see new possibilities for helping our women to get well and be made whole.

Endnotes

[1]Alice Walker, *In Search of Our Mother's Gardens*, p. 6.

[2]Peter Lord, *Soul Care*, Grand Rapids, p. 10.

[3]Thomas C. Oden, *Pastoral Theology*. Cambridge: Harper and Rowe, p. 187.

[4]"IBID", p. 187.

[5]IBID.

[6]Audre Lorde, *Sister Outsider*, New York: Crossing Press, p. 56.

[7]Howard J. Clinebell, Jr., *Basic Types of Pastoral Care*.

[8]Rosemary Radford Ruether and Rosemary Skinner Keller, *Women In America*, San Francisco: Harper and Rowe, p. 121.

[9]Carol Gilligan, *In a Different Voice*: *Psychological Theory and Women's Development*. Cambridge: Harvard VP, 1982.

Bibliography

Augsburger, David *Pastoral Counseling Across Cultures*. Westminster Press: Philadelphia, 1986.

Cade, Toni *Black Woman*. New York: Mentor, 1970.

Clinebell, Howard J., Jr. *Basic Types of Pastoral Care*. Nashville: Abingdon Press, 1966.

Chodorow, Nancy. *The Reproduction of Mothering*. Berkley: U of California Press, 1978.

Grant, Jacquelyn. *White Women's Christ and Black Women's Jesus*. Scholars Press: Atlanta, 1989.

Gundry, Patricia. *Woman Be Free*. Zondervan: Grand Rapids, 1977.

Kolbenschlag, Madonna. *Kiss Sleeping-Beauty Good-Bye*. Harper Rowe: San Francisco, 1979.

Lord, Peter. *Soul Care*. Grand Rapids: Baker, 1990.

Lorde, Audre. *Sister Outsider*. Crossing Press: New York, 1984.

Ogden, Thomas C. *Pastoral Theology*. Cambridge: Harper & Rowe, 1983.

Patton, John, *Pastoral Counseling: A Ministry of the Church*. Abingdon: Nashville, 1983.

Ruether, Rosemary Radford, and Rosemary Skinner Keller. San Francisco: Harper and Rowe, 1986.

Sandmaier, Marian. *The Invisible Alcoholics*. McGraw-Hill: New York, 1980.

Schussler, Florenza Elizabth. *Bread Not A Stone*. Beacon Russ: Boston, 1984.

Walker, Alice, *In Search of Our Mother's Gardens*. Harcourt Brac Jovanovich: San Diego, 1983.

Wilson Schaef, Anne. *Co-dependence Misunderstood--Mistreated*. Harper & Rowe: San Francisco, 1986.

Wimberly, Edward P. *African American Pastoral Care*. Nashville: Abingdon Press, 1991.

Pastoral Care in The Black Church. Nashville: Abingdon Press, 1982.

Eleanor L. Miller, M. Div, Garrett-Evangelical Theological Seminary, Evanston, Illinois, is currently employed as Employee Assistance Manager at the Mercy Hospital and Medical Center in Chicago, Illinois. For many years she worked as In-patient Clinical Coordinator for the hospital's substance abuse treatment center. Active in recovery and prevention circles, Eleanor teaches, lectures, serves as a resource person and does many seminars. An ordained Baptist minister, she currently serves as assistant to the pastor at Mount Zion Baptist Church in Evanston, Illinois.

Fear of Female

I would have thought
she might understand my search
for another way to
talk about God.
but
She slapped my womanist face
and told me to
shut up.

Valerie J. Bridgeman Davis
April 28, 1991

CHAPTER 2
Theological Implications of WomanistCare
Marsha Foster - Boyd

"Casting the whole of your care -- all your anxieties, all your worries, all your concerns, once and for all -- on God; for God cares for you affectionately, and cares about you watchfully." I Peter 5:7 - The Amplified Bible.

The words of a traditional hymn of the church ring out as one considers the theological implication of WomanistCare:

Does Jesus care when my heart is pained too deeply for mirth and song; as the burdens press and the cares distress, and the way grows weary and long?

Does Jesus care when my way is dark with a nameless dread and fear? As the daylight fades into deep night shades, does he care enough to be near?

Does Jesus care when I've tried and failed to resist some temptation strong; when for my deep grief I find no relief, though my tears flow all the night long: Does Jesus care when I've said good-bye to the dearest on earth to me, and my sad heart aches till it nearly breaks, is it aught to him? Does he see? OH YES, HE CARES; I KNOW HE CARE, HIS HEART IS TOUCHED WITH MY GRIEF; WHEN

THE DAYS ARE WEARY, THE LONG NIGHTS DREARY, I KNOW MY SAVIOR CARES (Graff, 1984)!

How could a God who loves me allow me to be treated this way -- to endure what I have had to endure? African-American women have shed briny tears over this theological issue since Christianity was introduced to our enslaved foremothers.   As womanist ethicist, Katie Cannon (1988:4) states:

Black women are the most vulnerable and the most exploited members of the American society. The structure of the capitalist political economy in which Black people are commodities, combined with patriarchal contempt for women, has caused the Black woman to experience oppression that knows no ethical or physical bounds.

The God of the African-American woman is, nevertheless, a God of redemption, liberation and healing, and this God (in Jesus Christ) can best be understood by African-American women as we investigate the meaning of "our" God within our own particular context -- from a womanist perspective.

African-American psychologist, Nancy Boyd-Franklin's book, Black Families in Therapy: a Multi-Systems Approach, makes a distinction between religion and spirituality and the roles they play in African-American family life in the chapter entitled, "Religion, Spirituality, and the Treatment of Black Families." Though not all African-Americans are members of the many organized religious bodies, Boyd-Franklin (1989:78) is quick to point out that:

...many Black people have been raised with and have internalized a sense of spirituality .... Training in the mental health fields largely ignores the roles of spirituality and religious beliefs in the development of the psyche and in its impact on family life. In the treatment of Black families, this oversight is a serious one."

As pastoral counselors and pastoral caregivers, an even greater . mandate is given to explore theological concerns and questions with those whom we serve. In order to understand what might be happening psychologically, it is imperative that one ascertain the role of spirituality and/or religion in the lives of the African-American women with whom one works. How have African-American women appropriated the presence or, at times, the apparent absence of God in their lives? "Does Jesus care...?"

Let us now examine the foundational elements of Womanist Theology as articulated primarily in the work of Womanist theologian Jacquelyn Grant. This examination is of critical importance as African-American women work toward the development of a holistic approach to Womanist pastoral care and pastoral psychology -- WomanistCare. To paraphrase Jesus' question to his disciples: "Who do African-American women say that the Son of Man is?" (Mt. 16:13)

The Primacy of African-American Women's Experience in Womanist Theology and WomanistCare

According to Jacquelyn Grant, African-American women must do theology out of the tri-dimensional reality, racism, sexism, classism, experienced in the church and in society. (Grant (1989:209)

She states:

> To ignore any aspect of this experience is to deny the holistic and integrated reality of Black womanhood. When Black women say that God is on the side of the oppressed, we mean that God is in solidarity with the struggles of those on the underside of humanity, those whose lives are bent and broken from the many levels of assault perpetrated against them.

Katie Cannon, also, stresses the important of understanding the historical context of African-American women as moral agents:

> More than two and a half centuries of chattel slavery, followed by another century of forced segregation, have shaped the context in which Black women then -- and still to this day -- make moral judgments and ethical choices. Throughout the history of the United States, the interrelationship of white supremacy and male superiority has characterized the Black woman's moral situation of struggle -- a struggle to survive in two contradictory worlds simultaneously, one white, privileged, and oppressive, the other black, exploited, and

oppressed (Cannon, 1988:6-7).

These Womanist scholars are indicating that in order to understand African-American women, one must begin by exploring the unique history of African-American women in this country as it has been impacted by racism, sexism and classism. If pastoral counselors and pastoral caregivers are to be effective in ministering to African-American women, the history of our sisters must be taken seriously in order to encounter their stories.

From a psychological perspective, African-American history includes the collective experience of African-American women from the African past through contemporary times, the tri-dimensional reality, but must also be inclusive of our particular regional, economic, familial and individual experiences.

In my article, "The African-American Church as a Healing Community: Theological and Psychological Dimensions of Pastoral Care", I examine several sources of African-American pastoral psychology: 1) the African background, 2) the experience of slavery in America, 3) contemporary African-American life, and 4) the African-American church, as well as the critical importance of the historic role of "community" in African and African-American life. One must take these collective experiences into account as one works with African-American women in discovering God's place and God's purpose in their lives.

The Importance of the Bible in Womanist Theology and WomanistCare

Just as Christianity and the Bible were used against our foreparents as a tool to perpetuate the holocaust of slavery; the Bible, was and is still used unfortunately, by some in the church to subjugate African-American women. African-American women, therefore, have had to continually re-interpret Christianity and the scriptures in the light of our own (Womanist) experience. I would concur with Jacquelyn Grant's (1989:211) assessment:

> Though Black women's relationship with God preceded their introduction to the Bible, this Bible gave some content to their God-consciousness. The source for Black women's understanding of God has been twofold: first, God's revelation directly to them, and secondly, God's revelation as witnessed in the Bible and as read and heard in the context of their experience. The understanding of God as creator, sustainer, comforter, and liberator took on life as they agonized over their pain and celebrated the hope that as God delivered the Israelites, they would be delivered as well... Though they were politically impotent, they were able to appropriate certain themes of the Bible which spoke to their reality.

Our African-American foremothers were adapt at re-interpreting the white preacher's incorrect interpretation of scripture as they reappropriated the gospel message in the light of the oppression they had to endure. African-American women today must certainly do likewise.

Writing for contemporary African-American women, Womanist biblical scholar Renita Weems (1988:8-9) says in her volume, *Just a Sister Away:*

> [The book] was written for those of us who are hungry ... to hear a voice you recognize ... [it] is the kind of book which irascible women, hungry for stories of women they can recognize and a God they can trust, could snuggle up with and rejoice when reading ... Although there has been a recent groundswell of literature by and about black women in the non-religious sector -- and we all benefit greatly when black women regain their voices -- the voice of black women religious writers has been strangely muted. Therefore *Just a Sister Away* was written unapologetically with African-American women in mind as a way of reminding us that we were not an afterthought to salvation....

From the perspective of WomanistCare then, it is clear that if the African-American woman sees her own history and experience reflected in the interpretation of the scriptures, her sense of self-worth and self-esteem will be enhanced and she will feel a strong sense of empowerment. Just as African-Americans were empowered by the rise of black consciousness and black theology in the 1970's and 1980's when murals of a black Messiah were seen on the walls of many African-American churches, African-American women are likewise empowered when fresh interpretations of scripture like those Renita Weems have offered. These re-interpretations cause African-American women to review and re-investigate our unique encounters as African-American women with Jesus. We can sing with fresh fervor, "... He walks with me, and he talks with me, and he tells me I am his own ...." We are, in a theological sense, reborn and can claim a new sense of our oneness with Christ.

Just as the role of scripture must be re-evaluated from a Womanist perspective, so also must the role of the African-American church. The African-American church has historically given mixed messages to women due to the sexism which has pervaded it. Women are affirmed as African-Americans in the church, but because of either legislated or traditional gender restrictions, have little or no authority in the hierarchy or power structure of many denominations. Though there are far more women then men attending and giving financial support to most churches, women have no voice, generally, in making decisions about how monies are allocated, nor are they represented proportionally on steward, trustee, or other decision-making boards. Women are free to prepare and sell dinners or chair programs or "annual days", but are prohibited from serving as deacons in many local churches and from being ordained in many denominations. Women are permitted to be ordained and to pastor churches in some denominations, but are refused "promotions" from smaller charges to "major" pulpits with the frequency and rapidity of male counterparts. These and many other mixed messages have caused great anguish among African-American women who love the church and want to remain faithful to it. Womanists ask: "Would a God who stands beside us as we gain freedom from slavery, racial oppression, and classism in the larger society stand against us as we strive to be liberated from the sexism found in the church? Certainly not!" As African-American women become empowered through Womanist re-interpretations of scripture and through the development of Womanist approaches to pastoral care and counseling in which the experiences and perspectives of women are articulated and affirmed, the status and role of African-American women within the church will necessarily be changed. "And before I'll be a slave I'll be buried in my grave...."

The Revelation of Jesus in Womanist Theology
and WomanistCare

There was a joke my mother told me in the mid-1960's which circulated in the African-American community during those years. It went something like this:

> The United States' space program had finally progressed to the point where they were sending the first astronaut to heaven. The trip had taken some days, and the re-entry into earth's atmosphere had been difficult. Thousands of media personnel from around the world were present at the "splash down" of the space capsule, waiting anxiously for their first glimpse of the astronaut -- the first person to ever see God and return to earth to tell what

52

God looked like. The astronaut exited the capsule and was standing before hundreds of microphones. "What did He look like?" The question thundered toward the astronaut in several different languages simultaneously. The astronaut looked sheepishly, almost apologetically, into the cameras and whispered, "Well ... SHE was a Negro."

One can imagine the response of an African-American audience in the mid-1960's (some thirty years ago) upon hearing the ironic punch line that God would be at once Negro AND female was completely unexpected. African-Americans of that day and especially African-American women relished the astronaut's bewildered reply!

Jacquelyn Grant has likewise challenged African-American men and women in her analysis of the role of Jesus in the Womanist tradition. Grant concurs with James H. Cone's description of the Jesus of our foreparents (Core, 1986). This Jesus is a radical liberator of African-Americans from the racism and oppression they experience on a daily basis. Grant, as we have indicated, focuses on the tridimensional reality of African-American women. Jesus was and still is for many our "all in all". Grant states:

...Jesus [is] the divine co-sufferer, who empowers them in situations of oppression. For Christian Black women of the past, Jesus was their central frame of reference. They identified with Jesus because they believe that Jesus identified with them... Jesus Christ thus represents a three-fold significance: first he identifies with the "little people," Black women, where they are; secondly, he affirms the basic humanity of these, "the least"' and thirdly, he inspires active hope in the struggle for resurrected, liberated existence (Grant, 1989:212 and 217).

The chorus of the hymn cited at the beginning of this chapter rings out: "OH YES, HE CARES, I KNOW HE CARES, HIS HEART IS TOUCHED WITH MY GRIEF!..." for many African-American women Jesus is God's complete self-revelation, God incarnate.

Grant, however, pushes us as did the astronaut. Not only is Jesus "the Black Messiah" -- God with us in our suffering as African-Americans -- but "Christ among the least must also mean Christ in the community of Black women... Christ not only as Black male but also Black female."

Grant goes on to quote William Eichelberger's re-interpretation of Isaiah 53:3-5 which begins: "He was despised and rejected by others; a man of suffering and acquainted with infirmity ... "[NRSV] Instead of the usual interpretation of this passage as a prophesy concerning Jesus as the "suffering servant", Eichelberger substitutes "she" -- meaning the African-American woman -- at every point in the passage where "he" is found. Though Grant views Eichelberger's categories as very traditional, she states: "Nevertheless, the significance of his thought is that he was able to conceive of the Divine reality as other than a Black male messianic figure

54

(Grant, 1989:218)."

Grant emphasizes the <u>humanity</u> of Jesus as the most significant aspect of African-American women's Christological understanding, Jesus viewed as human rather than primarily as male. In her view, though African-American theologians have adequately addressed the racism implicit in Jesus' "whiteness", they have not adequately addressed the sexism implicit in Jesus' maleness. Grant asserts:

> I would argue ... that the significance of Christ is not his maleness, but his humanity ... God becomes concrete not only in the man Jesus, for he was crucified, but in the lives of those who will accept the challenges of the risen Savior the Christ. For [Jarena] Lee, this meant that women could preach; for Sojourner [Truth], it meant that women could possibly save the world; for me, it means today, THIS CHRIST, found in the experiences of Black women, IS A BLACK WOMAN ... Christ challenges us to ask new questions demanded by the context in which we find ourselves [emphasis added](Grant, 1989:220)".

Grant pushes African-American women to examine the manner in which religious language and symbolism have been used as tools of oppression in the church. She challenges us to transcend the traditional oppressive Christology which emphasizes Jesus' maleness, masculine image be it either Black or White of the divine.

One can see that this emphasis on the masculinity of Jesus perpetuates certain stereotypes about women. Women "need" men to help them out of difficulty, that women are the "weaker sex" and need to be rescued, that women can't think logically and they have to ask men what they should do, etc. These stereotypes serve to maintain the oppression of African-American women.

Grant urges African-American women to develop a self-affirming "egalitarian" Christology, one that will be fully empowering. It's true that the maleness of Christ would be paramount. But if Christ is a Saviour of all, then it is the humanity -- the wholeness -- of Christ which is significant. [Grant: 1988, p. 219] She points to the theologies of our Womanist foremothers, Jarena Lee and Sojourner Truth, as they espoused this more liberating "egalitarian" Christology.

We must also hasten to add that neither Grant nor this writer are advocating a Christology which minimizes, ignores or negates African-American men, but rather one which views men and women equally and empowers them equally toward the total liberation of the African-American community.

I have uplifted three components of Womanist Theology which have been examined as expounded primarily in the work of Jacquelyn Grant: 1) African-American women's experience, 2) African-American women's use of the Bible, and 3) the revelation of Jesus Christ. The importance of these theological components has been stressed as they impact the lives of African-American women so that pastoral counselors and pastoral caregivers might more fully understand those African-American women whom they are priviledged to "sit with" in churches and counseling centers. Womanist theologians must continue to dialogue with Womanist pastoral counselors and pastoral caregivers in order to insure the continued development of an authentic, viable, holistic Womanist pastoral psychology. This is WomanistCare.

Endnotes

My Savior Cares; words by Frank E. Graeff, tune by J. Lincoln Hall. Included in the Bicentennial Hymnal of the African Methodist Episcopal Church. Nashville: The AMEC Publishing House, 1984.

Katie G. Cannon, *Black Womanist Ethics*, (Scholars Press: Atlanta, 1988), p.4.

Nancy Boyd-Franklin, *Black Families in Therapy: a Multi-Systems Approach*, (New York: The Guilford Press, 1989), p. 78.

Jacquelyn Grant, *White Women's Christ and Black Women's Jesus: Feminist Christology and Womanist Response*, (Atlanta: Scholars Press, 1989), p. 209.

Katie G. Cannon, p. 6-7.

To be published in the Fall, 1991 *Journal of Theology*, Tyron Inbody, ed. (Dayton: United Theological Seminary).

Jacquelyn Grant, p. 211.

Renita J. Weems, *Just A Sister Away*, (San Diego: LuraMedia, 1988), p. viii-ix.

See James H. Cone, *God of the Oppressed and A Black Theology of Liberation*, Second Edition,

(Maryknoll, NY: Orbis Books, 1975, 1986) in order to gain a complete understanding of Black Theology (USA) as delineated by Cone.

Grant, p. 212 and 217.

Grant p. 217-18.

Grant, p. 218.

Grant, p. 220.

Grant, p. 219.

Selected Bibliography:
African-American Women
Marsha Foster Boyd
United Theological Seminary, 1991

Boyd-Franklin, Nancy. *Black Families in Theraphy: A Multi-Systems Approach.* New York: Guilford Press, 1989.

Bryant, Cecelia Williams. *Kiamsha: A Spiritual Discipline for African-American Women.* Baltimore: Akosua Visions, 1991.

Cannon, Katie G.; Harrison, Beverly W.; Heyward, Carter; Isasi-Diaz, Ada Maria; Johnson, Bess B.; Pellauer, Mary D.; and Richardson, Nancy D. (The Mud Flower Collective). *God's Fierce Whimsy: Christian Feminism and Theological Education.* New York: The Pilgrim Press, 1985.

Cannon, Katie G. *Black Womanist Ethics.* Ithaca: Cornell University Presds, 1988.

Davis, Angela Y. *Women, Race and Class.* New York: Vintage Books, 1981.

Fabella, Virginia; and Oduyoye, Mercy Amba, eds. *With Passion and Compassion: Third World Women Doing Theology.* Maryknoll, NY: Orbis Books, 1988.

Giddings, Paula. *When and Where I Enter: The Impact of Black Women on Race and Sex in America.* New York: Bantam Books, 1984.

Gilkes, Cheryl Townsend. *The Black Church as a Therapeutic Community: Suggested Areas for Research into the Black Religious Experience.* The Journal of the Interdenominational Theological Center, Vol. VIII, No. 2, (Fall, 1980): 29-44.

Grant, Jacquelyn. *Black Theology and the Black Woman.* Black Theology: A Documentary History, 1966-1979. Gayraud S. Wilmore and James H. Cone, eds. Maryknoll, NY: Orbis Books, 1979: 418-33.

IBID. *White Women's Christ and Black Women's Jesus: Feminist Christology and Womanist Response.* Atlanta: Scholars Press, 1989.

IBID. *Womanist Theology: Black Women's Experience as a Source of Doing Theology, with Special Reference to Christology.* African-American Religious Studies: An Interdisciplinary Anthology, Gayraud S. Wilmore, ed. Durham, NC: Duke University Press, 1989: 208-27.

Hollies, Linda H. *Inner Healing for Broken Vessels: Seven Steps to Mending Childhood Wounds.* Joliet: Woman To Woman Publications, 1991.

Hooks, Bell. *Ain't I A Woman: Black Women and Feminism*. Boston: South End Press, 1981.

IBID. *Feminist Theory: From Margin To Center*. Boston: South End Press, 1984.

IBID. *Talking Back: Thinking Feminist, Thinking Black*. Boston: South End Press, 1989.

Hull, Gloria T.; Scott, Patricia Bell; and Smith, Barbara; eds. *All the Women are White, All the Blacks are Men, BUT SOME OF US ARE BRAVE*. New York: The Feminist Press, 1982.

Lewis, Mary C. *HERSTORY: Black Female Rites of Passage*. Chicago: African-American Images, 1988.

Malson, Micheline R.; Mudimbe-Boyi, Elizabeth; O'Barr, Jean F.; and Wyer, Mary; eds. *Black Women in America: Social Science Perspectives*. Chicago: The University of Chicago Press, 1988.

McAdoo, Harriette Pipes, ed. *Black Families, Second Edition*. Newbury Park, CA: Sage Publications, Inc., 1988.

Moraga, Cherrie; and Anzaldua, Gloria. *The Bridge Called My Back: Writings by Radical Women of Color*. New York: Kitchen Table: Women of Color Press, 1981.

Robinson, Christine Renee. *Black Women: A Tradition of Self-reliant Strength, Women Changing Therapy: New Assessments, Values and Strategies In Feminist Therapy*, pp. 135-44. Joan Hamerman

Robbins and Rachel Josefowitz Siegel, eds. New York: Harrington Park Press, 1985.

Rodgers-Rose, La Frances, ed. *The Black Woman.* Beverly Hills: Sage Publications, 1980.

Simms, Magaret C; and Malveaux, Julianne M., eds. *Slipping Through the Cracks: The Status of Black Women.* New Brunswick, NJ: Transaction Books, Inc., 1986.

Smith, Barbara, ed. *Home Girls: A Black Feminist Anthology.* New York: Kitchen Table: Women of Color Press, 1983.

Steady, Filomina Chioma, ed. *The Black Woman Cross-Culturally.* Rochester, VT: Schenkman Books, Inc., 1981.

Walker, Alice, *In Search of Our Mothers' Gardens.* New York: Harcourt, Brace, Jovanovich, Publishers, 1983.

Weems, Renita. *Just A Sister Away: A Womanist Vision of Women's Relationships in the Bible.* San Diego: LuraMedia, 1988.

White, Evelyn C., ed. *The Black Women's Health Book: Speaking For Ourselves*. Seattle: The Seal Press, 1990.

Marsha Foster Boyd is Instructor of Pastoral Care
and Counseling at United Theological Seminary in
Dayton, Ohio. She is an ordained elder in the
African Methodist Episcopal Church and serves on
the General Board of The Christian Church (Disciples
of Christ) and is a member of The American
Association of Pastoral Counselors. Marsha has
written several articles and conducted numerous
workshops and training sessions. She is completing
PhD requirements at Graduate Theological Union and
received her M. Div. from Interdenominational
Theological Center in Atlanta, Georgia. She is
married to Kenneth Boyd and the mother of one
daughter, Evette.

Do You Wanna Be Whole

She lay on a bed of pain
    holding her head, the throbbing pounding to the
rhythm of insanity, out of mindful distance of
Reason:

    He had beat her again -- and told her
she had asked for it.
    Laying there, she tried to recall
when she had made the request.

    The couch could have been her coffin
so paralyzed she.
    But the Prophet inside her soul cried out:
Do you wanna be whole?

    The furlong back to Reason is Infinity.
No one but the Prophet knows the way back.
    But the beaten brow knew
the Journey began with an Eternal No More.

Valerie J. Bridgeman Davis
October 23, 1991

CHAPTER 3

WomanistCare: Liberation and Responsibility
Jerri E. Bender Harrison

We begin with the pain...

One day, a little girl came home from school especially proud of herself. It had been report card day and she had received A's in all of her classes! Anxious to share her excitement over her accomplishments with her parents, she rushed home and burst through the front door yelling, "Daddy, Mommy, come here! Please! I got all A's on my report card! Come see!!!" Her mother and father arrived almost breathless moments later and took the report card in their hands to look it over and see for themselves what their child had done. Her parents, standing over her, looked down on her and said, "Why sweetheart, this is what we always expect of you..." Well-meaning words that were meant to encourage. But somehow, the heart of that little girl, that hoped only to hear "You're wonderful!", began to ache.

Perhaps it was here where the wound was inflicted and the pain started to grow...Perhaps it was here where she began to feel that even perfection was not enough...Perhaps it was here where she started to be intensely driven to do more and be more, hoping unconsciously that if perfection could not get affirmation that perhaps more than perfection would...Perhaps it was here where she began to question her values, asking, "What more must I do in order for someone to say that I'm O.K.?"...Perhaps it was here where external accomplishments became not only important to but necessary for her sense of self-esteem...Perhaps it was here where she became afraid to let anyone see less than perfection in her and so she became the artist who always painted the perfect picture for others...after all, if perfection could receive only little or no encouragement and validation, what would imperfection receive? Perhaps it was actually here where the jail door slammed shut and the bondage began...Even as I begin to write this chapter, the stories, the tears, the laughter, and joys and sorrows of so many African American sisters' lives cross vividly before my mind's eye:

> Stories of survival and pain...
> Stories of years of neglect....
> Stories of incest...
> Stories of raising babies alone...
> Stories of alcoholic mothers and fathers...
> Stories of an unending cycle of poverty...
> Stories of physical abuse from a mother's
> father's hand--where the hand that should have
> healed became the hand that hurt...
> And yes, stories filled also with love...

Inherent in the content of each of these stories of the lives of my Black sisters there can be found a common, although perhaps smothered or stifled cry for freedom. As our slave foreparents used to sing:

"Freedom, O freedom...freedom over me
'Fore I'd be a slave, I'd be buried in my grave
And go home to be with my Lord!
Freedom, O freedom...freedom over me!"

I believe that such a cry for freedom and liberation, no matter what the pain in each of our individual stories, is an innate part of our very souls.

This cry to freedom in the midst of pain can be found in the lives of the women whom we encounter everyday. But, we have learned that to wear such pain as an "outer garment" makes us too vulnerable and so we have learned that in order to survive that we must either cover the pain or bury it...And so we step out into the world with store-bought, cosmetic smiles and designer outerwear to help us paint the picture for the world that "everything is all right!" when we, and perhaps even they, know that this is not the case. We all wear a mask that covers our true selves and our pain. It is these covered, hurting women that we meet every day. And they are our mothers, our sisters, our best friends, our co-workers, our church committee members, our aunts, our cousins, our grandmothers, out enemies and yes, they are ourselves...

My task is to help us learn how to care for these women (and ourselves!) who do not yet know how to be free and to help us realize both our responsibilities and limitation as pastor, counselor, or simply perhaps as friend, co-worker or family member in walking with them toward freedom. We shall accomplish this task by looking at liberation/freedom not only psychologically but also personally, scripturally and historically. Together, let us journey into freedom...

LIBERATION

I hear the cries of my people...
Cries that rise from the very core of our torn and afflicted souls...
Cries, though sometimes muffled, muted or silenced
That are nonetheless present and pressing in their urgent plea for freedom...
I hear the cries of God's servant, Moses, crying "Let my people go!"
I hear the cries of God's people saying "How can we sing the Lord's song in a strange land?" and "Is there a balm in Gilead to heal sin sick souls?"
I hear the cries of our mother's, mother's, mother's as they cried out for relief and release as they slaved in the master's house...
I hear the cries of my Black sisters and brothers-too long abused, neglected and forlorn...
Cries for liberation and freedom that will NOT be silenced...
I HEAR THE VERY CRIES OF THE SOULS OF MY PEOPLE...

(Liberation Poem by the Author)

As a minister, I hear the cries of people's souls every day. This cry for freedom is as old as our history as a people that were enslaved and as new as our most present pain. The "Problem" with this cry for liberation is that it is one that cannot be easily satisfied. Because the cost of becoming free is very high...

For a Black woman, liberation is certainly nothing new, Harriet Tubman, our "Black Moses, " knew the cost of liberation because she lived out that cost in her own life. "Her reliance on the God who liberates the soul from hell parallels her belief in a God who liberates persons from material and social bondage (Wimberly, 1986:31): For Harriet Tubman it was not enough to simply be saved and free in her soul for herself. Her salvation caused her to desire liberation--in a total way--for all of her enslaved people.

As a people we have always loved and served the God who liberates us, mind, body, soul and spirit. This God is woven into the very fabric of our culture and heritage. In their book *Liberation and Human Wholeness*, Drs. Edward and Anne Wimberly describe "six basic levels of God's liberating activity that bring about human wholeness. They are: (1) liberation from personal sin and guilt; (2) liberation from social, economic, material and political oppression; (3) liberation from developmental, transitional, situational and psychological crisis and stresses that have the potential for blocking growth; (4) liberation psychosocially of persons from penultimate, proximate and finite world views that block growth toward wholeness; (5) liberation of community and interpersonal relationships to facilitate growth; and (6) liberation through cultural mediums such as ritual to help the community organize its activity around holistic and liberating values (Wimberly, 1986: 131)." Truly, the God we serve "makes us free indeed" (John 8:36).

In the midst of this wholistic understanding of freedom and the God of our liberation, the question still remains: "How do I become free and how do I help others in their quest to become free! And what does it mean to be really free?" For me real freedom is to not be enslaved to or bound by anything or anyone that hinders our growth toward wholeness. That which enslaves us or binds us either lessens or eradicates our ability to be free.

When I think specifically of the pastoral care of women I am reminded of and saddened, humbled and encouraged by the thousands of stories of women who have had to battle their way out of cycles of pain that were enslaving and binding them. Some of the everyday realities that can bind a woman and hinder her journey toward freedom are: incest, poverty, domestic violence, physical or sexual abuse, fear, racism, sexism, classicism, 'man hunger', negative body image, sin, "caretaking of too many (Hollies, 1990:85)" role expectation, childhood wounds that are yet unresolved and what Rev. Cecilia Bryant calls "woman-want: a house of my own, a quiet place, someone to cherish me"...(Bryant, 1991:32): i.e., anything that a woman wants but for whatever reason just can't have. If you ever see a sister who says that she thinks that she is ugly, you are not only seeing the result, perhaps, of a painful childhood or an incident that attacked the core of her esteem but you are also seeing the product of a society that intentionally seeks to aid us in feeling bad about ourselves.

What then shall we do? How can we as women in general and Black women in particular find our freedom? First, I believe that we must gain an even better understanding of the wider social milieu in which we are encased, in other words, seek to understand the broader society that seeks to shape us. Our society is one that teaches us to either anesthetize or bury our pain. Both of these methods are masking devices that hinder our freedom. If we use the "anesthesia" of drugs, overeating, alcohol, illicit sex, looking good on the outside, etc. we only cover our pain. If we choose to bury our pain rather than deal with it openly and honestly, we put ourselves in even more of a bind because anything that is buried alive will try to get out! If we bury our pain alive before it's resolved, we find ourselves reacting to others in ways we can't explain, we find ourselves being controlled by our emotions as opposed to our being in control of our emotions. Thus, society, if our only teacher, serves only to bind us further.

RESPONSIBILITY

An examination of the roles of God, the individual and the counselor in facilitating change in persons is the process of becoming free. Scripture focus: John 5:5-9

"...a certain man was there, which had an infirmity thirty eight years. When Jesus saw him and knew

73

that he had been a long time in that situation, said unto him, Will you be made whole? The afflicted man answered him, Sir, I have no one, when the water is troubled, to put me into the pool: but while I am coming, another one steps down before me. Jesus said unto him, Rise, take up thy bed, and walk. And immediately the man was made whole, and took up his bed, and walked..."

In the story of the man by the pool of Bethesda, I see encapsulated a reflection of many of the issues that a person must face who is bound and yet seeking to be free. For surely each freedom seeker must examine the following questions: How long have I been bound and why? Do I really want to be made whole? Whose responsibility is my freedom? God's alone? Mine alone? Someone else's? Or a combination of all three? What must I do in order to become fully free? Let us examine this passage of scripture further to discover some of the answers to these and other questions.

Imagine with me, the scene: The city is Jerusalem. The specific spot within the city is a pool by the sheep gate, called Bethesda, that has five porches. On these porches lay thousands of people-- all broken and bound. The Bible says that they were afflicted, blind, lame and withered. However, if I were to look at the scene with a contemporary eye I'm sure I'd also see in the midst of that broken multitude both women and men who'd been abused, neglected, abandoned, alcohol and/or drug dependent, incest victims, etc.-all waiting with the others for the troubling of the water so that they too might be the first one into the pool and thereby be made whole. Funny, that the Bible refers to the "troubling" of the water--for it is only when life, persons or circumstances begin to get stirred up, agitated or when pain reaches its peak, that we are urged, nudged or encouraged to seek those things that will make us whole and free. Often, though, we name the "troubler" anything but an angel! Nevertheless, in this story, whoever got into the water just after the "troubling" was made whole of their disease.

See and feel with me, the story of a man who'd lain by the pool, on his bed, for 38 years-always trying to be the first one in the pool but always failing. Imagine the utter despair and lack of hope that he must constantly feel because of having a problem for so long that he's tried but failed to change. Imagine the lethargy, listlessness and apathy that must have set in on him, that daily instructs him that he might as well just lie down, give up and stop trying because he obviously does not have the power to move himself or change this circumstances. Feel his despair...

Imagine how cutting and perhaps even cruel Jesus's question "Will you be made whole?" may have seemed to this particular man. Imagine the man answering back to Jesus, "Do I want to be healed? If only you'd seen me struggle time after time to get to that pool only to be thwarted by someone else. If only you knew how long I've been like this. If only someone would help. me. If only..." But Jesus did know and yet His question still echoed, "Will you be made whole?" For Jesus understood that a long-lasting problem can cause one to despair of life to such a point that one loses the ability to hope that any other state is possible. Jesus also understood and saw that for some persons, "illness" or being bound can deteriorate into a situation which becomes a crutch, that can get them attention and that will allow them to blame others for what is not right in their lives; i.e., for not being free or whole. And so this question, "Will you be made whole?" still stood.

The Bible does not tell us all of the inner workings of how Jesus did it, but we see the results: Jesus tells the man to rise, take up his bed and walk, and the man does it. Perhaps simply by gazing into the strong but compassionate eyes of Jesus this afflicted, inert man was empowered to do for himself what no one and nothing else has been able to help him to do: take up his bed and walk!

God's role
"...to set at liberty them that are bruised..."
(Luke 4:18)

From the above passage of scripture we can begin to understand God's role in facilitating our liberation in these four ways:

1)   "Our present healer." God is present for us at our exact point of need to bring healing if we will only open ourselves to God's power. Whenever the broken and bound of humanity are present, this is where Jesus is present--from the sheep gate to the psychiatric ward of the

76

hospital; <u>God</u> <u>is</u> <u>present</u> to heal us.

2)   "Our compassionate challenger." God is also present in our lives to begin to lovingly ask us those penetrating questions that often cut us. By "troubling" our emotional and spiritual waters God stirs us beyond lethargy, despair and pain to begin seeking our healing.

3)   "Our restorer of hope." When life has torn us down to the point where we can no longer see anything but the brutal reality, it is God who restores our hope and lets us know that our case is not closed and that the final decision has not yet been made!

4)   "Our empowerer." God dwells within us. God must remind us of the powerful resources that reside within us that we neglect to tap into. Therefore, God empowers and enables us to take up our own bed and do what we feel we could never do--thereby making it impossible for us to blame others or make them solely responsible for our freedom. Through God's strength, we can learn to do it for ourselves!

<u>The Individual's Role</u> ("Take up your bed and take off your mask!")

We wear the mask that grins and lies,
It hides our cheeks and shades our eyes,--
This debt we pay to human guile;
With torn and bleeding hearts we smile,
And mouth with myriad subtleties.

Why should the world be overwise,
In counting all our tears and sighs?
Nay, let them only see us, while
we wear the mask.

We smile, but, O great Christ, our cries
To the from tortured souls arise.
We sing, but oh the clay is vile
Beneath our feet, and long the mile;
But let the world dream otherwise,
we wear the mask (Morton, Huckson,
1975:500)!

From the above mentioned scripture and Paul
Laurence Dunbar's poem, "We Wear the Mask," we
can begin to understand the responsibilities of the
individual who is seeking freedom in the following
ways:

1) "Take up your bed": The bed symbolizes those
   areas of bondage in one's life that they have
   either been lying on (i.e., covering up) for years
   or lying on (not telling the truth about) for years.
   Through God we are empowered to take up our
   bed and walk--leaving behind that bed which
   contains the pain that has bound us for so many
   years.

2) "Take off your mask." It is a great risk to
   decide to be vulnerable, come out of hiding and
   self-disclose to another person or group of
   persons the secret that has caused one so much

shame and pain. It is precisely this risk that will facilitate liberation. One caution: <u>only</u> do this with a person or group that is 'nonjudgmental and nonshaming (Bradshaw, 1988:117)." If we take the risk and are made to feel ashamed, we will go back into hiding. It is important for Black women, in particular, to choose wisely whom we share our inner selves with because we are battling against a cultural restriction taught to us on our mother's knee, for what they believed was our protection, to "keep the family business in the family." We as Black women must often remind ourselves that "wearing the mask" and "keeping the family business" serve only to isolate and bind us.

3) "See, admit and become willing"
   - First, a person must <u>see</u> that they <u>are</u> bound and that they do have a problem.
   - Second, after seeing the problem, the person must resist the great temptation to avert their eyes and deny the problem. We must not allow ourselves to live in states of denial no matter how deep the pain. We must <u>admit</u>/acknowledge our bondage.
   - Third, we must have such a strong desire for freedom that it moves us to action. In other words, one must <u>become willing</u> to do anything and everything that will bring about liberation from bondage. "Anything and everything" may include: letting go of destructive, ingrained patterns; not being

afraid of and permitting both tears and anger; a commitment to one's own wholeness and a financial investment in oneself if one chooses to seek out a competent pastoral psychotherapist for counseling on the journey toward freedom.

The Counselor's Role

"(Humans) as a created being has the power to take a hand in the creation of (themself) by utilizing and fulfilling the potentials which God has placed in (them). There is a sense in which a person plays a decisive role in (their) own being and becoming through his decisions, commitments and loyalties. The resources for healing are within the person; the pastor does not place them there. The pastor must be aware of models which encourage (them) to take on responsibility which only another can exercise. They must grant to each person what they want for (themself), freedom to work out (their) own destiny. Such freedom will produce anxiety in both pastor and person. It is essential to the quality of life envisioned in the Bible (Wise, 34-35)."

Before we begin discussing the responsibilities of the counselor, I feel it is necessary to clarify that, in this particular chapter, when I use the word "counselor" I do not simply mean a psychologist or psychiatrist, but rather a person with expertise in pastoral counseling and/or pastoral psychotherapy. Pastoral counseling being the discipline that "utilizes a variety of healing (therapeutic) methods to help people handle their problems and crises more growthfully and thus experience healing of their brokenness. Pastoral psychotherapy being the discipline that utilizes long-term, reconstructive therapeutic early life experiences or by multiple crises in adult life (Clinebell, 1984:26)" In other words, this type of counselor has what Carrol Wise calls a "dual orientation (Wise, 25)" that is able to engage a person both religiously and psychologically. Having said that, the responsibilities of this type of counselor are:

1) Establish an atmosphere of trust. "On the level of relationship they are called upon not to do but to be. This manner of being with a person may itself communicate the values central to the Christian faith: genuine love, hope and trust (Wise, 28)."

2) Be an "enabler of spiritual wholeness throughout the life cycle (Clinebell, 1984:103)". Walk with a person throughout as many stages of life, not as the one responsible for bringing freedom but rather as a partner/companion on the journey.

3) To not be "timid about raising diagnostic questions regarding spiritual issues and the need for spiritual growth (Clinebell, 1984:117)". A person who willingly comes to a pastoral counselor is not only asking for help with their expressed problem but also for guidance in exposing the spiritual roots of their crises.

4) A willingness to be with a person in the midst of their pain--and to receive whatever that involves from the client: self-disclosure, tears, rage, etc.

5) A perpetual surveillance of one's own needs and issues so that 1) one can be sensitive when/if transference and countertransference occurs in the counseling relationship and 2) one can continue to take care of herself while caring for others.

6) Learn how to spiritually engage a person so that you can help them to find part or all of their story in the stories of the Bible. This can be particularly liberating for a woman who has only seen the bible as man-centered and yet has "hungered for stories of women they can recognize and a God they can trust (Weems, 8): in their own Bible. For example, if a woman is physically ill and seeking a healing you might point her to the story of the woman with the issue of blood; if a woman is a workaholic, you might point her to the story of Martha and Marry-Martha being the busy one and Mary being the one who chose to sit at Jesus's feet. If a mother is grieving over the loss of her child, you might point her to the story of the widow for whom Jesus brought her son back to life. Yes, helping a person to find their story in the scriptures can be a life--changing experience.

It is my hope that as we have looked at liberation

and responsibility throughout this chapter in a psychological, personal, historical and scriptural mode that we've learned that: 1) every woman has points of pain in her life's story from which they cry out to be free from all that binds or hinders their journey towards wholeness; 2) this cry for freedom is one that is wholistic in that it affects mind, body and spirit and 3) finding and living in this freedom is a co-partnership and shared responsibility between God, ourselves and a pastoral counselor.

May we continue <u>daily</u> to learn how to be free ourselves and help others in their journey toward freedom!

<u>Conclusion</u>
We end with the healing...

I am glad to report that the little girl that we spoke of in our introduction is grown up and becoming free. Perhaps because she has a husband who loves her unconditionally...perhaps because she has a child who loves just to <u>be</u> with her...perhaps because she is coming to truly understand God's grace--<u>unmerited</u> favor--in her heart and not just in her head...perhaps because the grown woman understands now that her parents only expected so much from her because they loved her and wanted the best for her...perhaps because she's started her own therapy not only so that she can be a better counselor but also a freer person...perhaps because she loves herself even more now, she is willing to risk, in safe places, sharing some of those parts of herself that are not "complete" and finding that she is still loved and received...perhaps because it <u>is</u> time for the healing and liberation to begin, the little girl is now a woman who is <u>learning</u> to be free...

But still the question remains: "Will you be made whole?"

Endnotes

[1]Edward T. and Anne S. Wimberly, *Liberation and Human Wholeness* (Nashville, TN: Abingdon Press, 1986), p. 31.

[2]Wimberly and Wimberly, ibid., p. 131.

[3]Linda Hollies, *Inner Healing for Broken Vessels* (Joliet: Woman To Woman Publications, 1991), p. 85.

[4]Rev. Cecilia Williams Bryant, Kiamsha: *A Spiritual Discipline for African-American Women* (Baltimore, Md: Akosua Visions, 1991), p. 32.

[5]Jay Martin and Gossie H. Hudson, eds., The Paul Laurence Dunbar Reader (New York, NY: Dodd, Mead and Co., 1975), p. 306.

[6]John Bradshaw, *Healing the Shame that Binds You* (Deerfield Beach, FL: Health Communications, Inc., 1988), p. 117.

[7]Carrol A. Wise, *Pastoral Psychotherapy* (New York, NY: Jason Aronson, Inc.), pp. 34-35.

[8]Howard Clinebell, *Basic Types of Pastoral Care and Counseling* (Nashville, TN, Abingdon Press, 1984), p. 26.

[9]Wise, op. cit., p. 25.

[10]Wise, op. cit. p. 28.

[11]Clinebell, op. cit., p. 103.

[12]Clinebell, op. cit., p. 117.

[13]Renita Weems, *Just a Sister Away* (San Diego, CA: Lura Media, p. viii).

Bibliography

Bradshaw, John. *Healing the Shame that Binds You*. Deerfield Beach, Florida: Health Communications, Inc., 1988.

Bryant, Rev. Cecilia Williams. Kiamsha: *A Spiritual Discipline for African-American Women*. Baltimore, MD: Akosua Visions, 1991.

Clinebell, Howard. *Basic Types of Pastoral Care and Counseling*. Nashville, TN: Abingdon Press, 1984.

Hollies, Linda H. *Inner Healing for Broken Vessels*. Joliet: Woman To Woman Publications, 1991.

Martin, Jay and Hudson, Gossie H., eds. *The Paul Laurence Dunbar Reader*. New York, NY: Dodd, Mead and Co., 1975.

Weems, Renita, *Just a Sister Away*. San Diego, CA: Lura Media, 1988.

Wimberly, Edward P. and Anne Streaty, *Liberation and Human Wholeness*. Nashville, TN: Abingdon Press, 1986.

Wise, Carrol A. *Pastoral Psychotheraphy*. New York, NY: Jason Aronson, Inc., 1980.

Jerri E. Bender Harrison, M. Div., Garrett-Evangelical Theological Seminary, Evanston, Illinois, is currently enrolled in their Doctorate of Ministry Program, Pastoral Counseling track. An ordained elder in the African Methodist Episcopal Church, she is assistant pastor to her husband the Rev. Peyton Harrison at the Wayman AME Church in Chicago. A renown preacher, Jerri ministers to all persons, and yet has a special ministry and care for women. Both a writer and musician, Jerri is mother to their son, Brandon and expecting her second child.

Them Women and Jesus

She sang, he kicked her ribs;
she sang louder her soul's delight.
He had already changed her life:
she bore gladly Immanuel.

O woman, He said, your faith is great,
she fought like a she bear for her whelps;
"Even the dogs feed on crumbs," she persisted;
He relented, and blessed her foreign faith.

She bowed low, knowing the crowd
unconcerned for her healing, only her lawful ways;
so she trembled:
'til Jesus returned the touch.
she was no longer afraid.

A mother-in-law lay lanquishing,
burning under the illness rage.
His touch, cooling; the fever left.
She, in turn, touched His needs with her service

She felt sensation, being known .
He touched her soul, deep, by the well
she poured out her life, no water
He met her, then she told his story

Her hair smooth travel worn feet.
She, thankful, caressed him;

he declared her deed the gospel's creed;
don't He said, tell the story
save in her memory.

They ministered to Him, them women;
out of their means, they comforted Him.
And when He lay on a cooling board, they brought
more spices to keep the ministry going.

CHAPTER 4
Wholeness For Care Givers
Delois Brown Daniels

Your world is as big as you make it. I know, for I use to abide in the narrowest nest in the corner, my wings pressing close to my side but I sighted the distant horizon where the sky line encircled the sea and I throbbed with burning desire to travel this immensity.

I battered the cordons around me and cradled my wings on the breeze then soared to the uttermost reaches with rapture, with power, with ease! (Georgia Douglas Johnson)

Though "your world", according to the black poet, Georgia Douglas Johnson, can be created with ease, I believe it is created with effort, sometimes much effort, efforts sustained through the encouragement and nurturing received from others as fellow Christians. Women must integrate their personal and Christian identities into a care-giving that is meaningful to adequately use themselves in relation to other people and their needs.

This chapter focuses on the role a group designed for care-givers can play in enhancing the ministry of womanist care-givers. The chapter discusses this role from a theological and a practical perspective, presenting the group as an arena for intentional Christian care-giving. The group provides space for each participant to be affirmed in her care-giving gifts, to examine how her theology informs

91

and misinforms her person and care-giving, and to explore how her personality defines care-giving. Christian growth is facilitated by the participant encouraging each other personally to locate specific Christian experiences such as grace, redemption, reconciliation and forgiveness in their lives. This naming theologically communicates the biblical teaching God reveals God's love in human relationships and that God uses people as channels of grace. Thus, the womanist care-giver must be in touch with herself, willing to be vulnerable in sharing with other women, and committed to offering honest assessment of others as well as herself.

The temptation to simply play the role of the "good Christian" must be resisted at all costs; a commitment to honest explanation is needed to reconcile one's past and present, both the painful and the joyous, within oneself; thus responding deeply, and not merely intellectually, to God's grace. Such an integration aids the person to be herself, furthering integrating where the superficial dominates. Above all, integration must be found in God, acceptance of human imperfection and God's faithfulness to us. Since we are not born whole, but called to be, integration, then, includes reconciliation with God. Integral to our creatureliness is one's relation to the Creator. The ultimate formation of the womanist care-giver then, involves being shaped by social factors, other people, and personal experiences in addition to grace.

Reconciliation begins with the reality that God loves all creation, especially each individual. For many African-American women God's love is not fully encountered because of the self-hate that society breeds within African-American women. When we realize, personally, with the help of other women, that God loves us, we are able to claim our uniqueness, our specialness, the goodness implied in God's creation of us and to love others more fully. One can love oneself in spite of her incompleteness, flaws, imperfections or societal ideals, allowing one to center her worth in God and not in personal achievement, race, gender or nationality. Thus, we can accept God's unconditional love and work towards loving unconditionally because, grace empowers us to take risks; risks in being vulnerable in relationship and risks in our actions. We can take risks because within grace there is acceptance of humanity, non-condemnation of failure and, where necessary, the forgiveness of sins.

Grace, which we have in reconciliation, allows us to reveal our full self because of God's acceptance. This frees us to express the truth of who we are, one who knows herself intimately and is not what others desire or even need her to be. The myths of the black super women, the dutiful daughter, the magnificent mother, the wonder-worker wife no longer need to define our identify; God can define it. Grace teaches us of God's faithfulness to us, even when we are not faithful to God. At our point of weakness, when we might not expect God's faithfulness, out of this crisis our relationship to God might be strengthened, not weakened; reconciliation on the level of self means having love for oneself, being able to celebrate who one is as a creation of God (Romans 8:1-2).

We can see that a social context like the family system, affects a person's growth and view of themselves within a larger context like the society. Our self-esteem can be undermined or affirmed by those around us. We are born with potential; we start with a negative or positive foundation that is developed as we grow older. We can continue with a negative self-image until a crises offers opportunities for intervention, for reconciliation, for the grace of God. The group can help the participants recognize when and how their self-image negatively affects their care-giving. When God uses the group to be a channel of grace, we become more of what God has called us to be as whole persons and women. Again, we are not born whole; we are called to be whole in Christ Jesus; we are born incomplete; we become what we encounter in life. Until we gain a knowledge of what we're called to be by God, we may become what society fates us at birth. With the knowledge of what we're called to be, we can go beyond the expectations of society, to be shaped by the Word of God. Even if we have a positive foundation there are crossroads where that foundation might be undermined, because we never reach a point of being finished, complete, thus, we're always born to be re-molded, and re-shaped. Like Jeremiah's potter illustration, human nature is clay to be shaped and reshaped.

Movement towards wholeness is defined by the fruit of the Spirit. Fruit is the attributes and qualities that are internally developed. Love binds together these qualities: goodness, faith, hope, truthfulness. Negative development robs us of claiming the gifts we have because we are blinded by others ideas, rather than God's ideal. This also blurs our vision of other people. If we can't love ourselves, we have difficulty loving and accepting others. Negative development narrows our world view. As love binds positive qualities, fear underscores the negative ones-- fear of failure, fear of not measuring up, fear of rejections, etc.

Reconciliation within oneself means coming to terms with our strengths and weaknesses, seeing our weaknesses as growing edges and not handicaps and our strengths as gifts and not as achievements. Reconciliation on the level of others, means accepting them as they are, not who we want or need them to be, as God accepts us. This is essential for care-givers. People must be met where they are, as is highlighted in Ezekiel 3:15, and we must encounter them not as a phantom, an invention of our imaginations, but relate to them authentically. Attempting not to make others what we want them to be frees them to teach us about life and about being human. This approach can be practiced and modelled in the group. We can learn and grow from a new perspective, dealing with them in their needs, and not our thoughts of their needs. This is an affirmation of the person, the person's gifts, our common humanity and our oneness in Christ. Likewise the group must work toward creating an atmosphere which allows each member to select and control much of the content of their participation. Most people are a bit bewildered and upset when they discover there are no experts except the group itself because the group helps each member to discover her attitudes, perceptions and longings.

The group leader should be experienced as a truthful, faithful, pastoral person in her relations with each member of the group. The group leader provides the members with a supportive arena to explore their fears, failures, growing edges, quandaries, successes and gifts as the group is formed. Acknowledging appropriately her own growing edges sends the message that she also is involved in the process. She must be a learner, unashamedly and continuously. Out of new insights the group offers her an excitement and freshness that serves her well in care-giving. Members might well adopt certain ways and qualities of the others in the group, qualities which come naturally to the individual, having proven to be effective. Modeling is invaluable because from each other the group models being pastoral, attentive listeners, confrontational care-givers, vulnerable and emotionally expressive. As each reflects critically about her style of care-giving, she learns not to imitate, but to recognize and learn from what others do well. This modeling enables, rather than disables, growth in care-giving and in one's life in Christ.

Central to the process is the formation of the group. Time reserved to lay the foundation of good group dynamics where each member shares some of her life story, growth as a Christian and goals in the group is indispensable. This self-disclosure is a major element in building trust in the group, the introduction of members and the group helping the group assist members strengthen their care-giving to discover commonalties in the midst of the differences. The group leader shares her own journey to signal that her membership is in the group, that she is a co-learner in partnership with them committed to the process and the group.

People relate to the group in different ways. An example that illustrates this was Ethel, a lay person, who had not developed the skill of reading non-verbal signals nor was she aware of when she was invading the space of others. This caused numerous problems. Her desire was to be in close relationship with others, yet her behavior brought the opposite response. Her behavior will be extremely problematic for her as an active lay person in the church. She displayed some of these personality traits when she attempted to defend her motives or rationalize her actions. Immediately the signals seems to say, "Handle with care, danger, explosive, keep out." Therefore, the group had to be sensitive to timing, interaction and direction in regards to her in order for her to learn. The group leader related to her with patience, which most people did not do because of her irritating traits, and with acceptance, rare responses to her behavior. Thus Ethel felt accepted. This trust relationship allowed her to "hear" the questions the group leader raised about her unfulfilled need and inappropriate demands for intimacy, misplaced affection, anger, and feelings of rejections. Of course, her intimacy issues were intertwined with the other issues -- basic trust, autonomy, intimacy--which had not been resolved constructively.

To sharpen the focus on ministry different learning exercises can be used. A crucial exercise is peer review. The group should schedule time to assess group and individual performance. This allows the group to examine its ethos, style, and group dynamics, and gives each peer an opportunity to voice their. assessment of an individual's performance and each person to pause and assess her own. During reviews the perceptions held by each member are acknowledged as commonly held, held by some, or singularly personal perceptions. Self-perceptions find great, little or no support; new perceptions of each members care-giving is also given, often affirming unrecognized gifts.

Once a member of a group, Janice restricted her participation in group to an observer, rarely entering the discussions herself. Outside the group her peers expressed concern that they did not know her well, exploring why this concerned them. Since the group understood sharing in each other's integration as part of the process, having covenanted to share in each other's growth, this was an important group issue as well as individual issue. Some peers felt they had been shortchanged in the group process. They explored how she had shortchanged herself and her care-giving by hesitating to solicit their feedback and the support of others. They also voiced their observation that her hesitance to participate actively blocked her from being present and discovering herself in the group as a care-giver. The group, adopting the caring confrontations approach I had modeled earlier, confronted Janice in a caring but accountable manner, enabling her to move from being an observer to a contributing member. Janice shared issues of isolation and rejection that were intertwined with her biological parents putting her up for adoption as a child. She was able to look at how these issues blocked intimacy in relationships. She discussed how her smiles were often a camouflage for her inner pain. She also confessed how she felt inadequate in ministering to them. We shared with her our feelings of inadequacy at times in ministry. She saw how her self-disclosure aided the group in discussing an issue that all shared. We reflected on what baggage we carry and it affects how we function in a group. The students were able to utilize the group to help each other through support, confrontation, self-disclosure and clarification. The objective of the group is not group therapy, focusing on psycho-dynamics; the objective is group reflection, focusing in ministry, specifically care-giving.

Another learning exercise which can be used is the verbatim. A verbatim is a transcript of a care-giving visit, a word-for-word and gesture-by-gesture account of what occurred during a visit. These verbatim allows for members of the group to "observe" how members provide care-giving. It is also an instrument to examine what a person does in care-giving.

Karen, a member of another group, presented

a verbatim on a patient, who had beliefs like Karen's discarded religious convictions. The group began to ask critical questions surrounding the pastoral visit and they asked Karen questions like: Did she hear a particular issue the patient was raising? Wasn't a particular response quite preachy? What was her feeling when she made a certain comment? Why didn't she follow-up on the specific comment? How was she trying to care for the parishioner? What were the biblical/theological issues if any, which informed the visit? As the group began to probe the verbatim they helped her evaluate her ministry to the parishioner. Until the patient care conference she had been unaware of the tenseness of her conversation with the parishioner. She was not in touch with how much her low tolerance of the parishioners beliefs had adversely shaped her responses to and attitude towards the gentleman. The group's questions expanded the discussion by helping Karen link some of her evaluate her ministry. The process of reflecting on how her personal history, attitude and values shaped her ministry, lead to a learning issue for the group, an issue of professional growth, learning together how to evaluate one's ministry in addition to an issue of responsible patient care.

The group was able to help Karen begin to see how her own personal history affected her caregiving. In the visit she had been deaf to the patient, hearing the past preaching a God of judgement and law more than the unspoken and spoken concerns being presented to her. Karen discovered her intolerance of the parishioner was of the same quality as those intolerances from the past which she now denounced. The group saw that as a result of the questions asked, responses given and observations by each other, that she and the group each discovered something about themselves and their ministry. Karen found hidden within her theology a judgmental attitude. She realized an area of her past needed to be reconciled in order to enhance her care-giving.

The group serves as a channel of God's grace for Karen, Janice and Ethel, providing space for them as care-givers to be honest about themselves and to experience support and nurture in their call to ministry of care-giving. Each of them serve as an illustration of womanist care-giving as an intentional activity, a product of continual practice of and reflection on care-giving as a learned activity. Womanist care-giving emerges out of the total being of a person--her identify, faith, history. It is a communal act: women giving to each other so that each can give to others beyond their circle. T h e poem by Georgia Douglas Johnson which opens this essay captures well the experience of womanist care-giving I have discussed. 1) A womanist care-giver embraces the sisterhood, making her world bigger, 2) She must accept the challenge to participate in enlarging the world of the recipients of her care-giving 3) Finally, and most importantly, she must also enlarge her own inner world, finding it to be wonderful space carved in God's loving grace.

Bibliography

Cannon, Katie G., *Black Womanist Ethics*. Atlanta: Scholars Press, 1988.

Cooper-Lewter, Nicholas C. and Mitchell, Henry H. *Soul Theology*. San Francisco: Harper & Row, 1986; pp. 112-113.

Harkness, Georgia. *The Ministry of Reconciliation*. Nashville: Abingdon Press, 1971; p. 52.

Hunter, George I. *Supervision and Educating - Formation for Ministry*. Cambridge: Episcopal Divinity School, 1982.

Nowen, Henri. *The Wounded Healer: Ministry in Contemporary Society*. New York: Doubleday, 1972.

Russell, Letty. *Changing Contexts of Our Faith*. Philadelphia: Fortress Press, 1985; pp. 17-20.

Russell, Letty. *Human Liberation in a Feminist Perspective - A Theology*. Philadelphia: Westminister Press, 1974; pp. 106-113.

Delois Brown-Daniels, M. Div., Yale School of Divinity, currently heads the Clinical Pastoral Education Program at Northwestern Hospital, Chicago, Illinois. An ordained American Baptist Pastor, she is Associate on the staff of Trinity United Church of Christ in Chicago. A reknown preacher and teacher, she has conducted numerous seminars, workshops and retreats, as well as run revivals and stirred hearts as Woman Day Speaker across the country. Delois is a certified supervisor in the American Association of Clinical Pastoral Educators and a fellow in the College of Chaplains. She is married to Dr. David Daniels and mother of one son, David, Jr.

To The Rhythm of Linda

Regal woman

   who dances with trees

      in the grace of sunshine --

   when the music stops,

      oaks bow in reverence

to your queenly self.

Wrapped in purple

   who sings with wind

      in the mercy of starlight --

   when the chord ends,

      Orion smiles in awe

at your royal presence.

Someplace in ETERNITY the music and song keeps

ringing in Sovereign applause.

Valerie J. Bridgeman Davis
April 27, 1991

CHAPTER 5
Options for WomanistCare
Linda H. Hollies

And I thought the mountain had moved! The mountain in my life had began its growth in my early childhood as a victim of incest by my father, a minister. The mountain had no name, but started to appear in the night, silent, unbidden and formidable. The mountain grew with each passing day, shame and confusion formed its base and its widening girth was to have far reaching effects in my life.

Violence against women and children is a mountain in the midst of the Church. Statistics prove that one out of four women is a victim of some type of violent abuse in this country. What is frightening and angrying is that approximately every ten minutes a female is being sexually attacked by a close relative or family friend and every three minutes the attack is being done by her own father. It makes no difference whether the abuse is sexual, psychological, emotional, physical or spiritual. All abuse begins the growth of a mountain in a human life.

I grew chronologically, inspite of the mountain standing tall and looming large in my life. I learned how to "act", wear roles and smile in order to hide my aching heart and wounded spirit. I went to church, functioned professionally and appeared to have it all together. But years after the sexual assaults to my physical person had ceased, the mountain was yet in control. I denied the pain, stuffed the shame and evaded dealing with my father, or confronting my mother. For large mountains are too much for one individual to handle alone. From early childhood I learned to internalize the guilt, work hard to be perfect, fantasize about my parent's love for me, and hoped that my dreaming, wishing and pretending would impress the mountain into going away!

Chipping at the mountain meant acquiring a college education. Digging around the mountain meant marrying my childhood sweetheart, having a family, buying a home and keeping up with all the "social" norms and expectations. Picking away at the mountain meant seeking a personal relationship with God, naming myself as the guilty one and trying to accept the forgiveness and grace I was taught about. And still, the mountain did not disappear. I simply became more adept at moving around it.

Life has a way, a manner, even a habit of providing victims with the opportunity to choose different avenues of exploration. Facing mid-life, I felt called to leave my professional career in industry and entered seminary. In the midst of a mid-life crisis I had to select new patterns of dealing with the issues in my life which continued to cause me daily pains and nightmares. I was tired of dancing around this same mountain. I wanted to face it squarely, speak to it and watch it disappear. For does not the scripture declare that with faith, the size of a mustard seed, I could "speak to this mountain, be moved to another place, and it shall move; and nothing will be impossible for you." (Matthew 17:20)

The Chinese character for crisis is also the same symbol for opportunity. My mid-life crisis took me to Garrett-Evangelical Theological Seminary, in Evanston, Illinois, at the age of forty-three. I was a wife, mother of three, an established career woman, who dared risk everything to seek God "fully" in order to have God help me move this mountain! As an Africian-American female, with the "herstory" of incest in my life, I approached seminary with some illusions, fantasies and hopes. I believed that in this place of spiritual illumination and theological education I would be led to great insights and truths about my inner pain. From class to class, course to course, seminar to workshop, I sought diligently for someone, something to help me examine my mountain. Foolish woman that I was! Seminaries are not prepared to teach you how to map out mountains as a cartographer, nor are they equipped to teach you how to examine mountains as a geologist. Seminaries, I soon found out, are established institutions that perpetuate the silence of the status quote in regards to mountains and mountain movers.

There was not one class, not one professor who was willing to engage with me, from a Biblical base, in the exploration of my mountain. I was a student, a number, one to be helped throught the system, but not helped by the system with tools, methods or principles to assist me in becoming a mountain mover. I was simply "a certain woman". And, the mountain did not move!

During my second year of searching, seeking and struggling through seminary, I attended our chapel service in observance of Christian Unity Week. Joseph Cardinal Bernadin, the leader of Chicago Catholics, stood to deliver his message. When he stood, a group of women from the seminary community also stood. They did not stand in unity with the Cardinal, but they stood in unity for a common purpose, symbolizing the oppressive treatment of women in the Catholic Church. They remained on their feet, in the audience, in front of him and, in the choir behind him, during his entire homily on "Unity". He never gave any indication that he saw anything amiss during this service. He completed his message and took his seat. All of the women sat down. Our president came to the podium, concluded the service, making no mention of having noticed these women doing anything out of the ordinary. The services concluded and life in the seminary went on. And so did the pain of women.

The matter did not die, the issue was not settled. Male professors approached the president and dean, seeking some sort of appropriate measures to take against women/students/leaders of local congregations, who were not "hospitable" to the Cardinal. Some talked of writing to their bishops, telling of their rebellious natures. Some of them even talked of expulsion. Finally, a community open forum was held to address the issue of hospitality. Not one seminary official made mention of the pain of the women. Not one approached the group to say, "I see your pain and I realize that your anguish is authentic."

This is the reality of the seminary. This is the reality of the institutional Church at large. This is the reality of our society in regards to the abuse, neglect and pain that is continually perpetuated against women and children. This segment is not really heard, their plight is never fully addressed by individuals being prepared for professional ministry. Seminaries are truly "inhospitable" to those who enter with mountains in their life. They become "non-persons" within those hallowed halls.

This incident gave me great focus and clarity as to just how much the Church and the seminary had failed me, a victim of domestic violence in both my childhood and adult life. For I realized that not only was I a victim of incest by my father, but the "hushed", secret and quiet atmosphere of the seminary made me a rape victim of the Church! As I sat in that chapel service I realized that seminary education is primarily focused on white, male western European values. None of these categories fit my life!

The abuse in my life, which formed the mountain, which controlled me even after his death, was caused by a male parent, trained in interpreting a male God who was powerful, threatening, vengeful and the Creator of mountains! If anything, seminary reinforced this image of "the male God", with a predominately male administration, staff and faculty. The core courses, required of all students, were taught, for the most part, from a male centered focus and bias. Any course with curriculum focused on the eradication of violence against women and children, was held at the urging of female focus groups, and seldom would you find a significant number of men registering or attending.

The Church, as an institution, and the seminary, as its training ground, are primarily concerned with the perpetuation of the status quo, which is white, male hierarchy. Where was the hospitality for me, an African-American, female, who was "a stranger in a foreign land"?

My soul yearned for answers. I felt the mountain closing in on me. My spirit was perishing for lack of nurture, affirmation and acceptance. My hope was diminished in this sacred place that offered me no help with my mountain climb/search/watch! Seminary could not handle the crisis of a woman of color, who lived daily in the presence of a mountain of evil. My classes in theology did not deal with my theodicy and my personal search for answers to help me in order that I would be prepared to help others like myself.

In the middle of my crisis, feeling that I was living on the edge, seminary offered me the opportunity to explore Clinical Pastoral Education (CPE). The process for taking this hospital based course required three counseling sessions with The Center For Pastoral Care. Clinical Pastoral Education forces you to encounter your inner self, probe your past and scout around the mountains in your life. With fear and trembling I attempted to tell "most " of the truth of my past by revealing that I was a physical abuse victim. I was too ashamed to name the sexual abuse, for the white male pastoral counselor might not understand! However, I passed the assessment sessions and was allowed to enter CPE where I began to investigate and acquire additional information about me and my mountain. CPE made me a mountain scout. And even CPE has its boundaries when it comes to mountains like mine! However, the movement that I made in CPE caused me to think that the mountain had moved!

My CPE Supervisor, Beth Burbank, was willing and determined to see me find a reconnaissance agent who was trained in exploring this mountain at its base. Peggy Garrison, a white, female, student, moving on her Ph.D. in Religion and Psychology, offered to become a geologist with me. She took her pick and rope in hand, and we began to scale the mountain.

Scaling a mountain is a tremendous task, requiring months of preparation, deliberation and determination. Peg and I did good work together, picking, chipping and digging away at the many layers of painful shame which lay at the base of my present rage and anger. But, two years is not long enough to work through a mountain as huge as one with forty years of growth and spread. I graduated with honors, from seminary, capable and prepared "they said", ready to go into the local parish and become a mountain mover for others.

Off I went to face the Conference Board of Ordination, degree in hand, willingness in head, fear in my heart, for my own mountain was yet alive, not quite as hugh, but alive, nevertheless. For I have come to understand that mountains do move as you name them and speak to them as your own! But, they move as you move further away from them with growth, development and acceptance of the past.

I was raped by the Board! My theology was attacked, my anger became an issue, and my vision for ministry as a full-time pastoral counselor was crushed. Knowing that I must proclaim and teach from my own experiences, I tried to help them see that my anger stemmed from my mountain, and the mountain would always be in my life. The examination group took on the dynamics of my family of origin. There was a violent parent who took the lead in the abuse, a silent parent who pushed back against the wall, and several non-verbal and non-rescuing siblings! As a candidate, I was both different and powerless. In that room I became a victim of the system. On that day I watched the mountain take on new dimensions in the Church.

After the rape of my personhood was complete, the "family"wanted to pray for me. I was aware enough of the growing mountain, prepared enough by my days of therapy and professional enough to refuse their prayers and walked out of the room with my head held high! I was in control, not the mountain! They were shocked, surprised and angry. But, I would not lie down and be a willing victim of violence by another system. I would not enter the duplicity of silence and I would not perpetuate the family "lie". And certainly, I would not be controlled through their prayers!

I do believe in prayer. Prayer is a powerful

force which connects me with a God who cares, understands, guides and empowers me to act in the future. It is my understanding that when prayer ceases, living must be done. Prayer has been used against survivors to keep them silent, humble, submissive and "in their place". My God has given me more tools to utilize as I pray, work and continue to speak to the mountains and to those who erect them. My God is an AWESOME God, full of power, balanced by love, who provides me strength to take a stance against anything or anyone who attempts to cause mountains to block my life.

In her book, *Struggle To Be The Sun Again*, Asian theologian, Chung Hyun Kyung, writes for herself and many other women of color: "my learning...did not help me to discern the activity of God in my people's everyday struggle. Instead, it was the student movement that enabled me to see the false ideology embedded in my formal theological education. Deconstruction of every aspect of theological imperialism became a main focus in my theological work. I decided that I would not waste my life solving the theological puzzles of the people who were the cause of our suffering; I wanted to spend my energy debunking their theological imperialism and studying (my) people's history and culture as I listened to my people's inner voice, in their struggle for survival and liberation....for the master's tools will never dismantle the master's house". (introduction, p.3. Orbin Books, Maryknoll, New York, 1990).

The realization crept in on me that I had to do

theology from my own experiences of mountains, pain, anger, shame and guilt. For too many years I had tried to hide the mountain in my life. But a mountain is part of my life story, a major force in my walk of faith. To ignore the mountain, was to ignore my struggle too find God in, around, beneath or at the foot of it! Finally, I understood that the "stuff" of the mountain could be used to help me to speak to it and move it!

My new reality meant talking about my mountain to those who did not want to hear. But, in speaking out, I put a voice to millions of untold stories. My speaking led to my writing about the shame that had held me bound to the mountain for too long. The writing led me to conferences, retreats, seminars and ADVANCE, where I was able to make sense out of the non-sense of our lives for many other survivors. The workshops meant digging into scriptures from a new perspective and then preaching and teaching with another voice!

I have found that as a daughter of a loving God, who is not bound to the gender of my father, I have rights and privileges. I have the right to be delivered and made whole. I have a right to be freed from the demonic spirits which kept me at the foot of that mountain, chained in pain for so many years. I searched until I discovered that the covenant decreed that Jesus was my Shalom and that I could be made whole. My digging uncovered that my shame and my pain did not have to remain in control of my life and that if the mountain didn't want to move, I could.

Clinical Pastoral Education, therapy and my

personal life of faith began to utilize the mountain as the place to begin sharing my story. Wisdom allowed me the time necessary to comprehend the fact that my hurt and my pain held the potential for the unique and beautiful within me to be released. With time for renewal, refreshing and revival I moved away from the mountain in order to get a new view. I came to understand that God's original intent for my life was to be a blessing to the Kingdom. Even though evil had been permitted to touch my life, invade my space and erect a mountain, the original intent remained. My former fears turned into compassion. My destructive rage and anger was changed into a hunger and thirst for wholeness. And my perfectionist tapes were changed to new tunes of "let me tell you how to scale a mountain!" And day by day new instructions have been played, through prayer and meditation.

Climbing a mountain is never a once and for all time event. For new mountains are yet being created, and old mountains are intact. However, learning to do theology from the underside, the backside or even on the side of the mountain gives new hope and courage in the God of mountains. My God has called me to be that "virtuous woman" of Proverbs 31. Truly, this sister-girl was a mountain mover and shaker who did many things well. As a younger woman, I felt that this chapter spoke about a little, soft-spoken, docile woman, dressed in white, whose honor came from knowing how to be submissive to her "man" who set in the council of elders at the gate. Searching for new tools, methods, implements and equipment to help move my mountain, led me to understand and to experience that she was an ISCHAR CHAHIL. This Hebrew term means a woman of strong force, courage and tenacity. Her perseverance and strength to climb over, go through or simply walk around and away from obstacles and mountains to achieve her status, spoke to me in a new way. She fulfilled her destiny and became one of the many women in the Old Testament who refused to let mountains dictate her life and life-style. Today, I realize and accept the fact that I am called and compulsed to be a "virtuous woman"!

On this side of the mountain, from a different vantage point, I thank God for the journey of examing my mountain. My journey has enabled me to talk about the painful effects of domestic violence to other sisters, and free them to speak of their own experiences. My journey has forced me to write about my journey, once again, to share my points of wholeness which will encourage other sisters to keep digging and shoveling away. My journey with the mountain forced me to seek out help in order to become a helper; to search for comfort in order to become a comforter and to become a storyteller for those who cannot yet speak.

The mountain is a part of my life. The mountain is not in control, but it is a piece of my "herstory" which impels me, motivates me and assists me in reaching out, speaking out and doing ministry with other women. The mountain caused me to form a para-church group, WOMAN TO

WOMAN MINISTRIES, INC., which provides both education and support for women of color and lets them know that mountains do exist and that you can choose to move!

Seminary and the Church would receive a failing grade when it comes to making mountain-movers. And yet, seminary forced me to continue seeking for answers to the missing piece. Seminary taught me that faith was living, experiencing, reflecting and acting with God, who is very real and very present, even inspite of mountains. I learned how to "do" theology in seminary, with all of its confining and limiting boundaries. For Church History especially taught me and gave me an appreciation for wrestling with truth, as we understand it. I continue to wrestle with my own truth as I learn how to make space and room for myself in the Church of the Living God.

I am an ordained elder in the United Methodist Church, a product of a seminary with a fine reputation and a quality faculty and I am a survivor of these systems of sameness, which is an idol god! God said to the wandering, chosen people of Israel long ago, and to the victims and survivors of violence today, "You have been circling this mountain too long, it's time for you to turn..." (Deuteronomy 2:3) Mountains won't move easily, but, Sister-Friend, you can move, you will move and you MUST!

Bibliography

Bankston, Majory *Braided Streams* (San Diego: Lura Media, 1985).

Burkhardt, Walter, S.J. ed., *Woman in a New Dimension* (New York: Paulist Press).

Caprio, Betsy, *Woman Sealed in the Tower* (New York: Paulist Press, 1982).

Chung, Hyun Kyung *Struggle To Be The Sun*, Orbis, New York, 1990).

Christ, Carol, *Diving Deep and Surfacing: Woman Writers on the Spiritual Quest* (Boston: Beacon Press, 1980).

Christ, Carol and Plaskow, Judity, *Womenspirit Rising* (New York: Harper & Row).

Clark, L. Ronan, M. Walker, E, *Image Breaking, Image Building* (New York: Pilgrim Press, 1981).

Gilligan, Carol, *In a Different Voice: Psychological Theory and Women's Development* (Cambridge, MA: Harvard University Press, 1982).

Greenspan, Miriam, *A New Approach to Women and Therapy* (New York: McGraw-Hill).

Haughton, Rosemary, *The Re-Creation of Eve* (Spring, Ill: Templegate Publ.).

Hull, Gloria *But Some of Us Are Brave,* Feminist Press, NY 1982.

Cooper, J. California *Some Soul To Keep*, St. Marton Press, NY 1987.

Fortune, Marie *Is Nothing Sacred?* Harper & Row, NY 1989.

Scott, Patricia Bell, *Double Stitch: Black Women Write About Mothers and Daughters*, Beacon Press.

Glaz, Maxine *Women in Travail and Transition*, Fortress Press, Minneapolis, 1991.

Schaff, Anne Wilson *Woman's Reality* (Minneapolis, Minn: Winston Press, 1985)

An Inclusive Language Lectionary, Cycle (A, B & C) (Cooperative Publishing Assoc., Atlanta, New York, Philadelphia, 1984)

Sanford, Linda & Donovan Mary Ellen, *Women and Self Esteem* (Harrisonburg, VA: Penguin Books, 1984)

Linda H. Hollies, M. Div., Garrett-Evangelical Theological Seminary, Evanston, Illinois, is senior pastor of the Richards Street United Methodist Church in Joliet, Illinois. An ordained elder in her denomination, she spent two years as a resident and supervisor in training in Clinical Pastoral Education at the Catherine McAuley Health Center in Ann Arbor, Michigan. Author of *Inner Healing for Broken Vessels, Restoring Wounded Warriors and Womanist Rumblings*, she has contributed to several books and numerous magazines. Married to Charles H. Hollies, she is mother to sons, Greg and Grelon, and daughter, Grian. She is grandmother to Giraurd Chase.

Rocka My Soul

I cain't, Janie Mae, make it widout chu, I know
dis true.
    I cain't stop awonderin' out loud hows' the
worl' ever make it well --
    widout Folk to hang to. Somebody's gotta hold
me up, 'cause
    I cain't lean well on a Nothing Post.
We needs each others, Janie Mae, dis true.
    Twan't never meant to make it alone.
Menfolks dun tol' de lie of the bootstraps --
    us women knows its a line in the sto'm
biggr'n bootstaps and pullin' long mor'n one at a
time.
    its clear to me, Janie Mae.
Widout chu, my soul's barren, 'lone and sad.
    My soul needs the hum of a sista singing no
ways tired as I drag my weary feet.
    Promise me, Janie Mae, you'll learn
how to rocka my soul,
    and when it's your turn, I'll be the post.

Valerie J. Bridgeman Davis
November 25, 1991

CHAPTER 6

Establishing Women's Ministries
As WomanistCare
Roberta Lockett-Collins

Sisters are hurting!

Carroll A. Wise defines pastoral care as meeting people at the point of their needs (Wise, 1966:8). As an African-American woman, I am deeply in touch with the needs of African-American sisters. I have walked, talked, cried, prayed and worshipped with them as we studied together at Chicago Theological Seminary. I have grieved with them, held their hands, and consoled them during my seven years as hospital chaplain. I have buried our sons and daughters who have dies from overdose, gunshot wounds, AIDS and other illnesses.

As I write this chapter, a host of sisters come to mind. Mary comes to mind. Mary was ordained by a host of male and female clergy, including one of her seminary professors. She was later told by her Baptist pastor that her ordination was null and void at the church where she had been a member since childhood. Several years have passed and Mary still has not been accepted as an ordained minister at this church. When I talked to her recently, I could still hear the pain in her voice as she recalled this experience.

I remember Gayle. Gayle uprooted her family, left her family and friends to journey to a small town in South Dakota to serve an all white congregation as one of its associate pastors. She was the first black and first woman to serve in this position. After serving for a short time, Gayle was isolated and rejected by many of the white women in the congregation. This was very painful. She left after a year to return home to find employment and a place to live. She is waiting for another assignment from her denomination. A year has passed and Gayle is still waiting and hurting. Her eyes swell with tears as she recalls this experience.

I will never forget Vivian. Vivian ended up in the hospital after selling chicken dinners in her church basement for two days. This has been her "place" in the church for years. Vivian said to me, "I wish God had more significant places in the church for women to work." I learned from talking to Vivian that women at her church had to get permission from their male pastor to visit other churches. Women were not allowed to wear dresses above the knees, nor jewelry, lipstick, pants or anything "pertaining to a man" in her church.

The names have been changed, but the characters remain the same--African-American women. They are the characters portrayed in Frances Beal's article, Slave of Slave no More: Black Women In Struggle:

As a black, she had to endure all the horrors of slavery and living in a racist society; as a worker, she has been the object of continual exploration, occupying the lowest place on the wage scale and restricted to the most demeaning and uncreative jobs; as a woman she has seen her physical image defamed and been the object of the white master's uncontrollable lust and subjected to all the ideals of white womanhood as a model to which she should aspire; as a mother, she has seen her children torn from her breast and sold into slavery; she has seen them left at home without attention while she attended to the needs of the offspring of the ruling class (Beal, 1981:16-17).

Haunted by the memories of past experiences, visited and re-visited daily by racism and sexism on the job and in their churches, concerned about their futures, sisters are hurting. The basic "heart hungers" or needs of every individual are to be loved, affirmed, and accepted. Where do women go seeking to get these needs met? Listen to the voices of African-American sisters:

...when the cracks of the past begin to ache, strain, and pull at my guts, it's a sister, a woman, whose right-brain thinking allows her to "feel" with me instead of the left brain male, who wants to immediately offer a solution...when you are in pain, you need comfort and understanding. When you are hurting, advice is not the answer (Hollies, 1990:77).

...When our backs are against the wall; when we feel abandoned, abused, betrayed, and banished...we need a woman, a sister who will see in our destitution a jagged image of what one day could be her own story. (Weems, 1980:7)

African-American women, like other women, have always turned to each other for support and comfort. Women throughout history have seen the need for women support groups and ministries. In 1895 Josephine St. Pierre Buffin, an African-American woman, in her speech addressing the First National Conference on Black women cited:

We need to feel the cheer and inspiration of meeting each other. We need to gain the courage and fresh life that comes from mingling of congenial souls. We need to talk not only on things which are of vital important to us as colored women, but also the training of our children...and I have left the strongest reason for our conferring together as to last. All over America there is to be found a large and growing class of earnest, intelligent, progressive women, who are leading useful lives, and are only waiting for the opportunity to do so, many of them warped and cramped for lack of opportunity, not only to do more, but to be more (Lerner, 1972:p.).

My story parallels the stories of many African-American sisters. I share portions of that story so that other sisters will know that no matter how deep the wound, how great the pain; there is hope. I experienced racism at the age of six when I was told by a white waitress to get off a counter stool where I sat eating ice cream with a white playmate. I attended an all black school where only my light-skinned sisters were used as cheerleaders and in the leading roles in school plays. It was in the black schools that I got accustomed to hearing "if you are white, you are right; if you are brown, stick around; and if you are black, get back." At both school and home I remember being called ugly, because of my "kinky" hair and brown skin. At age 13 I began working in a white woman's home eight hours a day for $2.00 a day or $15.00 a week. I remember my grandmother who worked for discarded clothing, household items and left-over food. I know what it means to ride the back of Greyhound and Trailways buses and searching for a place in back of the bus station so that whites could not see me empty my bladder. I know what it means to be rejected, abused and knocked to the floor by a husband who thought it was right to beat a woman. Thank God, I was able to get out of that situation alive. I have experienced the pain that comes from being rejected and isolated by the good church sisters and a pastor who said I was crazy if I thought God called women to preach. The pastor told me a womans place is in the kitchen and bed. This was a church where I had worked for twelve years selling chicken dinners in addition to organizing the Sunday School and Youth and Children ministries, as well as working as church secretary. Hurt, bitter, angry and on the verge of a mental breakdown, I left that church. My self esteem

126

was at its lowest. I felt bound on the inside. It was during this period that I began to seek out women's ministries. In my search I found many, but not one ministered to my spirit as did ministries under the umbrella group of Universal Foundation for Better Living, headquartered in Chicago, Illinois, especially the Johnnie Coleman Institute where I continue to take classes. These ministries include the Christ Universal Temple Church, one of the largest or possibly, the largest African-American congregations in the city of Chicago. The Johnnie Coleman Institute is the teaching ministry of the church, and it was in these classes that I began to grow and unfold mentally and spiritually. The founder of these ministries is an African-American women, Dr. Johnnie Coleman.

Some years later I discovered Woman to Woman Ministries, Inc. an inter-denominational Sisterhood for women of color. Women from various Christian ministries, various denominations and various cities and states make up the membership in this group. Woman to Woman Ministries, Inc. encompasses women of all backgrounds and professions: clinical psychologists, chemists, teachers, pastors, evangelists, state employees, personnel directors, RN's, chaplains and more. The group holds an annual conference with seminar sessions, workshops and sharing groups (Hollies). It is the care of sisters involved in these ministries that has kept me growing and unfolding and moving toward healing and wholeness. The primary goal of all pastoral care--and all ministries should be that of

127

liberating, empowering and moving people toward wholeness. Carroll A. Wise says that pastoral care is more than a ministry to persons in crisis. It is also a ministry to persons at the point of growth (Wise, 1966:68). In the Johnnie Colemon Institute classes are designed to meet people at whatever stage of development they are in. In pastoral care it is important to meet people at the point of their needs. The Coleman Institute and Woman To Woman Ministries utilize the practices of consciousness-raising, inclusiveness, listening, sharing, and referring, as intentional pieces of their program format.

<u>Consciousness-raising</u>:

The focus of consciousness-raising is primarily to get people to know themselves. Many African-American women, like other women, need to know who they are. This should be the overarching goal of all women's ministries. Women have adopted the attitudes of culture, viewing themselves as naturally subordinate (Clinebell). Many women need to know that the Divine Presence inhabits their beings as it does all of humankind. In God, we all live, move and have our being. In the classes at the Institute students are asked to affirm who they are. The affirmation that is used to help students focus on their oneness with God is: I am a child or manifestation of God, and every moment God's life, love wisdom and power flow into and through me. I am one with God, and I am governed by God's law (Coleman,). In this ministry, affirmations and denials are called the tools for consciousness-building. Linda Hollies, Executive Director of Woman To Woman Ministries, Inc., encourages women to use affirmations also. She cites in her book *INNER HEALING FOR BROKEN VESSELS*: Affirmations replace the negative statements we too often make to ourselves...Our minds cannot hold or process two thoughts at the same time...positive affirmations can program out negative, self-critical thoughts. Whenever or wherever you find yourself being self-critical begin to affirm who you are, a wonderful, unique individual.

African-American women need to praise and compliment each other more often. A hug, a praise or a compliment is an affirmation. Even caring confrontation can serve as an affirmation. A confronter is one who nudges, urges, pushes you to take yourself by the nape of the neck and get on with dealing with your issues. A confronter challenges you to be in charge of your life and gives you honest feedback that can assist you to see your proper perspective (Hollies, 1990:2) As African-American women we need to lift each other up. Consciousness-raising is a concept used in the women's liberation movement. The four stages as used in this group process are:

Opening Up - Women are encouraged to open up and tell their life experiences as women...in an atmostphere of support and acceptance of feelings This results in group closeness and mutual support.

Sharing - Women are encouraged to share their deep feeling, needs and experiences. This leads to an awareness that their problems are rooted in society's problems more than in their individual inadequacies.

Analyzing - The group reaches, beyond personal experiences and focuses on their devalued position in society. This leads to a new subjective understanding which is integrated with the group members personal experiences as women.

Abstracting - The group members evolve a new

vision of their potential as women, and the group begins to see itself as a means for changing social institutions so that the potentials of women can be realized more fully (Clinebell, 1984:)

At my first Woman to Woman Ministries Advance, I was in a group facilitated by Rev. Jessica Ingram, an African-American woman, who co-pastors with her husband. She opened up and shared her story and encouraged the other women in the group to do likewise. As women shared stories and life experiences, a real bonding took place among the women. As we discussed and analyzed our concerns and issues, we began to see that the sexism we experience in our churches and the racism we continue to experience in America have roots in the devalued positions of African-American women during slavery. As Renita Weems cites: "Slavery was abolished in America a mere one hundred twenty five years ago; but evidently one hundred twenty years is not long enough to abolish the memories and attitudes that slavery arouses in a nation." When I arrived at the conference, I felt alone in the challenges I was facing in my ministry, a small congregation I had founded a few years prior. When I left, I realized that other African-American women were experiencing similar challenges. We affirmed one another and when I left Advance, I left with a new vision and new hope.

African-American women's consciousness can also be raised by reading books authored by African-

American women. Renia Renita Weems (1988:9) writes: *JUST A SISTER AWAY* was written unapologetically with African-American women in mind as a way of reminding us that we are not an afterthought to salvation...

Women's ministries could start reading groups, where women can come together to read and discuss books by African-American women and other authors that affirm their worth as women. Pastors can start reading groups in the church for the purpose of consciousness-raising among women and men and other church groups. Seminarians can start using the resources of their school library to compile a 'must' reading list for women. I recall a young woman who was deeply depressed because her husband had walked out of their marriage. I immediately remembered the stories of African-American women in *INNER HEALING FOR BROKEN VESSELS*. After we talked, I told her I would like to give her a copy of this book. She called me two days later to let me know how meaningful this book had been to her. She said she started to feel better after reading it. She relates that she saw herself in the book over and over again. She is already in therapy. She is now ready to seek out women's support groups.

In Women's ministries where consciousness-raising is taking place...

- women are affirming themselves and each other
- women are opening up and sharing their innerselves
- women are sharing their stories

- women are reading the writings and stories of other women.

Inclusiveness:

Inclusiveness is an acid test for African-American women who want to know if their consciousness is raised to that level of oneness with God, a level where they know that if this is true with them, it is also true for other African-American sisters. As African-American women we come from various denominations. Whether we are sanctified, filled with the Holy Spirit, speaking in tongues as the Lord gives utterance, or baptized in "Jesus" name only, immersed in a pool or lake, or sprinkled from the baptismal font, we must remember we are all sisters. Our paths may lead us along different routes, but they all lead to God. Women who are planning to start new women's ministries groups should be inclusive. Sisters are hurting whatever their religious orientation. More often than not, they are experiencing sexism in their churches and most certainly racism in society. Let us remember the characters in the stories are African-American women whether they are Baptist, Methodist, Pentecostal, Lutheran, Presbyterian, Muslim or of other religious orientation. Our struggle is not against our denominations. The struggle as quoted from Harley and Tarborg-Penn has been against sexism, which all women have experienced. It has been against racism, which black men and women have experienced. The struggle has been compounded because at times white women created barriers to achieving the goal of equality for black women. Other times black men stood as obstacles to the black woman's struggle.

As Clinebell cites, women who are awakened to their full womanness and liberation issues are the best leaders of women groups.

Listening:

Many times women just need a listening ear. Many times as I ministered to grieving women and families in my hospital ministry, I said very few words. A ministry of presence and listening is much needed. Families have called me back to say how much they appreciate my just listening to them. Often times when people are hurting, recited prayer is not the answer. The first stage of grief is shock, and in shock, I find that people are not ready to pray. Women's ministries should be "listening place". At the 1991 Inner Healing Advance sponsored by Woman to Woman Ministries at the University of Michigan in Lansing, Michigan, sisters were up most of the night listening to concerns and issues that their sisters brought to the conference, but small groups were listening places, also.

We need to learn to listen to the pains of our sisters.

> Listening is much more demanding than it is ordinarily supposed, since it involves much more then just hearing and registering words, sentences, and ideas...listening means becoming aware of all the cues that the other emit,...one does not listen with just (her) ears; (she) listens with (her) eyes and with (her) sense of touch;

(she) listens by becoming aware of the feelings and emotions that arise within (her) self because of contact with others (that is, (her) own emotional resonance is another "ear"), (she) listens with (her) mind, (her) heart, and (her) imagination...(she) listens to the messages that are buried in the words encoded in all the cues that surrounds the words...(she) listens to the sounds and the silences...listens not only to the message but also to the context...

Total listening...encompasses all the cues emitted by the other (Clinebell, 1984:311)...

At Advance, the listening skills of the pastoral counselors, chaplains, social workers, pastors, therapists, were at work, as they listened for the "real issue" following an angry outburst by one of the women. Sisters were willing to listen otherwise, sisters would have gone back home with all the pain bottled within.

The Johnnie Coleman's ministries has a prayer ministry. People may call for prayer or to have a "listening ear" on the other end of the phone. As a pastor, many times I have been up studying late at night, the phone rings and I know that it is someone who needs a listening ear. There have been times the person did not tell me who they were and talked on and on before finally saying "thanks for listening." Many times, on the evening shift at the hospital, people who had lost a loved one to death would call needing a listening ear. Women's ministries should always provide space and time for listening on their agenda at conferences and gatherings. This can be done in small groups or as a one-to-one ministry. Group facilitators should always be available for one-to-one ministry.

Referring:

Women's ministries should be places where referrals are made when needed. Women with little or no experience in substance abuse counseling should know where persons can go for help. Women who have been sexually assaulted should be referred to counselors who have expertise in this area. The resource list of women's ministries should always include battered and abused women shelters, community mental health councils, alcohol and drug treatment programs, AIDS support groups and bereavement support groups for infants, children and adults. Properly conceived, referral is a means of using a team effort to help a troubled person. It is a broadening and sharing, not a transfer of responsibility (Hollies, 1990:80).

Recommendations for Future Ministries Within Existing Women's Ministries

Women's ministries should minister. During a one-week period in my hospital ministry, I ministered to the families of five little girls, one as young as seven years old, who were sexual assault victims. And as I shared Hollies book *INNER HEALING FOR BROKEN VESSELS*, many young women who had been victims of incest came forth. Is there a way that women's ministries can address this situation? Perhaps incest and sexual assault could be the topic of a dialogue group. Could we provide ministry to young girls at our conferences? Mothers and grandmothers could bring their children and grandchildren. If we could stop even could one young girl from being the victim of incest or assault, we would have accomplished much. Mothers need to know what to look for if they suspect sexual assault in the home. As I have shared with other pastors at conferences, I have noted that female pastors are in need of other sisters to share issues about their common ministry. Many female pastors are struggling with small congregations. Perhaps they could come together to pool resources and energies, share funding sources and proposal writing. Perhaps we could share approaches and ways to minister to "groups" that form within our congregation to thwart our efforts. Many of these groups are women, our own sisters. How do we get them to work with us rather than against us? How do we address the issue of members in the congregation who still find it hard to relate to a woman pastor?

Woman to Woman Ministries, Inc. and the Johnnie Colemon's ministries have been sources of strength and inspiration to me. They have provided the strength that keeps me growing and unfolding. I highly recommend the further establishment of additional Women's Ministries to stop the needless hurting of African-American sisters. We can be made whole!

ENDNOTES

Wise, Carroll A. *The Meaning of Pastoral Care* New York: Harper and Row, 1966, p. 68.

Beal, Francis M, *"Slave of Slave No More: Black women in Struggle* The Black Scholar 12 November/December 1981, p. 16-17, reprinted from Wol. 6 (March 1975).

Hollies, Linda H., *Inner Healing for Broken Vessels: Seven Steps To Healing Childhood Wounds*, Joliet: Woman To Woman Publications, 1991.

Weems, Renita, *Just A Sister Away*, San Diego, CA: LuraMedia 1988, p. 7.

Lerner, Gerda, *Black Woman In White America* New York: Pantheon Books: 1972.

Hollies, Linda H., *A Pamphlet About Woman to Woman Ministries*, n.d.

Clinebell, Howard, *Growth Groups* Nashville, TN: Abingdon p. 77.

Coleman, Johnnie, *Basic Truth Principles Lesson Plan*.

Hollies, Linda H., *Inner Healing for Broken Vessels: Seven Steps To Healing Childhood Wounds*, Joliet: Woman To Woman Publications 1991, p. 91.

Clinebell, Howard, *Basic Type of Pastoral Care & Counseling: Resources For The Ministry of Healing & Growth* Nashville, TN: Abingdon, 1984).

Weems Renita H., *Just A Sister Away*, San Diego, CA, LuraMedia, 1988, p. 7.

Harley, Sharon and Tarborg-penn, Rosalynn, ed., *The Afro-American Woman; Struggles and Images* Port Washington, NY: Kennikat Press, 1978, p. ix.

Hollies, Linda H., Inner Healing for Broken Vessels: Seven Steps To Healing Childhood Wounds, Joliet: Woman To Woman Publications, 1991, p. 82.

Clinebell, Howard, *Basic Type of Pastoral Care & Counseling: Resources For The Ministry of Healing & Growth* Nashville, TN: Abingdon, 1984)p. 311.

BIBLIOGRAPHY

Albanese, Catherine L. and Stein, Stephen J. *Sisters of The Spirit*, (Bloomington; Indiana, University Press, 1986.

Barbach, Lonnie Garfield, *For Yourself - Fulfillment of Female Sexuality*, Garden City, NY: Anchor Press/Doubleday, 1979.

Bogin, Ruth, *Black Women In Nineteenth-Century American Life* University Park, Pa.: Pennsylvania State University, Press, 1979.

Bonhoeffer, Dietrich, *Life Together* New York: Harper & Brothers, 1959.

Butterworth, Eric, *Discover The Power Within You* New York: Harper & Row, Publisher, 1986.

Cannon, Katie G. *Black Womanist Ethics* Atlanta, GA: Scholars Press, 1988.

Chapian, Marie C. and Coyle, *Free To Be Thin*, Minneapolis, MN, 1979.

Clinebell, Howard, *Basics Types of Pastoral Care and Counseling-Resources For The Ministry of Healing and Growth* - Revised and

Enlarged edition (Nashville, TN: Abingdon Press, 1984).

Clinebell, Howard, *Growth Groups* Nashville, TN. Abingdon: 1970.

Harley, Sharon, et. al, *The Afro-American Woman, Struggles and Images* Port Washington, NY: Kennikat Press, 1978, ix.

Hooks, Bell, *Ain't I A Woman: Black Women & Feminism Boston*, Mass: South End Press, 1981.

Kitzinger, Shelia, *Woman's Experience of Sex* New York: Penquin Press Books: 1983.

Lerner, Gerda, *Black Women In White America,* New York: Pantheon Books: 1972.

Leslie, Robert C., *Sharing Groups In The Church* Nashville, TN: Abingdon Press, 1979.

Mac Haffe, Barbara J., *Her Story* Philadelphia: Fortress Press, 1986.

Mollenkott, Virginia Ramey, *Women, Men and the Bible* New York: The Crosswood Publishing Co. 1988.

Morgon, Ruth, *Sisterhood is Powerful* New York: Randon House.

Morton, Nelle, *The Journey Home* Boston, Massachusetts: Beacon Press, 1985.

Reuther, Rosemary Radford, *Mary-The Feminine Face of The Church* Philadelphia Westminster Press, 1977.

Reuther, Rosemary Radford, *Sexism and God-Talk: Toward A Feminist Theology*, Boston: Beacon Press, 1983.

Warch, Williams, *The New Thought Christian*, Marina del Rey, CA: Devorss & Company, Publishers, 1977.

Weems, Renita J. *Just A Sister Away*, San Diego, CA Lura Media, 1988.

Wise, Carroll A., *The Meaning of Pastoral Care*, New York: Harper & Row, 1973.

Van Den Berghe, Pierre L., *Race and Racism: A Comparative Perspective* New York: Wiley, 1967.

Roberta Collins, M. Div., The Chicago Theological Seminary, has spent the last seven years of her life as Chaplain at St. Bernards Hosptial in Chicago, Illinois. Ordained in the Baptist Church, she pastors the Christ Center of Truth, Chicago, Illinois, which she founded. An organizer of womens retreats, Roberta hosts several institutes each year which features education, training and motivation through speakers, workshops and seminars. Married to Robert Collins, she is the mother of Justus LaDarrell and grandmother of DeJuana and DaShauna.

Recognizing

Just a Flash

Still

Someone inside peeked
    from behind the pain

and

you knew her --
It was not the smile,
    nor the way she held her head sideways;
It was not the flow of her dress,
    nor the way her hair resisted the wind;
Just a Flash

Still

she peeked out and you said, "hi."

Valerie J. Bridgeman Davis
April 6, 1991

CHAPTER 7
Support For The Grieving
Janette Chandler - Kotey

How do I support someone going through grief? This is the question that we as ministers often ask. The answer to this question is so complex that one can only begin to answer in the context of a brief overview, hoping to expand our concepts of grief.

Before exploring support to the grieving, grief deserves a description. It is such an elusive, and individualistic state that often goes undetected and unaddressed. It would be safe to say that grief is a process, which is usually, by definition slow and painful. The grief process is characterized by necessary adjustment to significant changes in a person's life over which they had little or no control (like death, divorce, or loss of job).

We, as human beings, often fear intense experiences that we cannot predict or direct. Grief fits this category of intense individualized experience. Subsequently, grief is often categorized as dysfunctional behavior to be avoided or hidden, rather than a part of our normal and necessary adjustment process. Added to this natural process are the expectations of the religious community who view grief as dysfunctional and whose biblical quotations and beatitudes may suggest that a Christian's grief process ought demonstrate the "eternal hope": resurrection, heaven, rewards, kingdom reign, etc.

Although the stages of grief are generally classified as five stages, shock, denial, anger, guilt and hope, the length and depth of grief varies according to each individual. The first principle of pastoral care for the grieving is the rule of individuality. Each person handles their grieving process differently; in fact, no two people handle it alike. Although general principles may apply (i.e., denial, anger, bargaining, etc.), variations within the broader stages remain numerous. Personality traits, age, experience, belief, financial status, and other factors influence the ways the grieving process will express itself. The pastor should keep in mind that each case is unique.

The compassionate pastor understands that grief is experience physically, mentally and emotionally.

WHAT IS GRIEF?

Grief is the emotional and physical response to loss which affects every individual. Physically, the feeling is much like an unpleasant emotion caused by awareness of danger or an acute enduring pain. Sympathy triggers a stimulation of the nervous system; consequently, sweating, increased flow of blood, reserves of energy grows and digestibility takes more than the usual time. Stages of emotion range from alarm to disbelief and denial to remorse, anger and guilt. Behavioral response to grieving is largely determined by one's cultural environment.

Recognition of one suffering from grief should be detected by an observant caregiver.

WHAT IS GRIEF REACTION?

Symptoms associated with suffering pain or hurt

due to a loss may be classified as a complexity of psychological and somatic symptoms. Psychologically, one reacts to generalized awareness such as, mental anguish, discomfort caused by feelings of mental pain, inability to function in organized activities, restlessness, bitter regret, tribulation and remorse. Somatic reactions affect the physical functions of the body-shortness of breath, and tightness in the throat area. Reactions may occur immediately following the crises and often the severe hurt may act more slowly, depending on the relationship and the status of the involved persons.

Four to six weeks, and sometimes longer are average times before most acute grief actions begin adjustment. This is particularly true for sudden or unexpected death.

Whenever individuals exhibit behavior which does not appear to be adaptive for the time and the grief, professional counseling services should be recommended in order to prevent morbid reactions, both physically and psychologically.

Grief is not always as obvious as in cases of sickness and death. Grief can express itself in subtle ways in the case of divorce, failures or job loss.

Those who experience divorce mourn the death of a living relationship with their spouse. Divorce terminates a relationship just as abruptly and completely as death does. A divorced woman benefits from a similar approach in pastoral care. This sister too needs the same transitions through the stages of grief for her wholeness. Some have even reported that divorce is worse than death because they may actually see that person again though the relationship is dead! In these cases the anger we experience is actually a part of the grief process.

Reverend Andrea Bishop, Pastor of a United Methodist Church, found legitimate grieving often takes place in cases of amputation or loss of body parts. If we return to our initial definition of grief: necessary adjustment to significant life changes like death or divorce, it becomes easier to view loss of limbs or of both internal and external body parts, like a womb or breast, as causes for grief and opportunities for pastoral care. It is also essential in ministering to women that we don't neglect the grief of miscarriages, abortions and oftimes, the inability to conceive.

Broadening the concept of grief in terms of the sources of grief can help the church recognize more of the hurting among the membership. Those parishioners who have relatives who are seriously ill or dead get their names in the bulletin and they are discussed among the membership. The more dutiful among the laity will call on the telephone, visit the homes, attend the funeral, etc., but those who have a friend that is recently divorced or laid-off from their job, are not considered among the grieving. They should also be considered as grieving!

Grief education which describes and legitimizes grief is the first aid in ministry to the grieving. The pastor can coordinate and inform the interested parishioners and the immediate family and close friends of the major tenants of the grieving process. They should expect the process to last for several months and attempt to help with necessary duties and kindness. More sophisticated efforts should remain with the pastor and professional counselors.

Psychological reactions are perhaps most significant to pastoral care. The pastor should not be reluctant to refer parishioners to a good physician in cases where medication and treatment may prove helpful. The appeal to God for help and the assurance of the scriptures that God is a present help in time of trouble is the important contribution of Christian faith in the time of crisis.

The grief of parishioners has been an opportunity to lead them into a better devotional life. By reading with them the selected passages of scriptures, particularly from the Psalms, the individual who is experiencing grief becomes comforted with the knowledge of God's love and support. Soon the parishioner associates their comfort with devotional readings and prayer.

Some of the parishioners with whom this pastor has worked through the grief process have shown an increased knowledge of the scriptures and a greater appreciation for the work of the church. Occasionally, a period is allowed for personal testimony where some have stated that through their time of sorrow and loss they have come to know God in a more personal way. They spend more time with God--in prayer and meditation. This demonstrates the beauty of pastoral care. A Christian can grow stronger through the grief process when coupled with the comfort of friends, the church, scripture and prayer.

A great part of intense grieving can often be traced to theological sources. In a majority of cases I find that a poor understanding of salvation's reward - eternal life, or even questions about the actual existence of God can contribute to the mourner's sense of abandonment and helplessness. Unscriptural ideas about the nature and character of God often contribute to "secret anger" at God, which prevents the mourner from making necessary transitions to the next stage of grief. These present unique opportunities for the pastor and parishioners to encourage deeper faith.

The mourner may harbor guilt, or remorse over acts, conversations, or even thoughts which were not in the best interest of the deceased. A good listener, with a few appropriate words of wisdom may often help this person deal with "20/20 hindsight".

Grief provides a theological platform for the sovereignty of God. God is the Creator of the Christian family. Being Creator and Lord of the events of the Christian's life, one may conclude that catastrophic events which cause grief have been allowed to occur. The understanding is that "it" could not occur if God did not permit it to occur. The old theological question arises, "If God is good why does bad things happen to good people?" But, the scripture does not say that all things are good, only that "all things work together for good for those who love God, for those who are called according to God's purpose." This pastor believes that the events which cause grief in the lives of Christians remain under the Lordship of Christ. God uses the terrible events as well as the good events of the Christian's life in order to establish that "purpose" in the life of the Christian.

Faith, by definition, requires believing in God beyond the present circumstances. What is the purpose for God's will in the Christian's life? How does this particular grief contribute to the overall purpose which God has planned? Only time and prayer can answer these questions. Only faith can substitute for the answers until they are seen clearly. "Faith is the substance of things hoped for and the evidence of things not seen." When Christians walk through a time of darkness they hold to the faith that God is yet in control in their life and that good will result from the present evil. There remains no substitute for faith in these circumstances! Encouragement and consolation help the person grieving to hold to the Christian faith but not substitute for faith. This "challenge" to their faith in God will help strengthen them over a period of time, which many testimonies of other Christians can prove.

Jesus was accustomed to the grief we experience. Some dismiss Jesus' emotional expression as not the same as what we experience. By underscoring His divinity they minimize his humanity. But when Jesus agonized in the Garden of Gethsemane, or when he wept over Jerusalem, or was grieved at the unbelief of the people--what He experienced was genuine grief. There is no sin in grief. This message is taught and practiced at St. Luke's U.M.C. Everyone will experience grief at some point in life. Christ was "acquainted with grief and sorrow" as reported in Isaiah 53; therefore, "He is touched with the feelings of our infirmity." This pastor directs the attention of the grieving person to the suffering of the Savior: both His passion and His resurrection. To avoid the guilt often associated with "a lack of faith" because a spirit-filled Christian feels grief and anguish, the example of Christ's own grief proves helpful.

Because of a dysfunctional view of grief, the process may cause particular conflict for those of charismatic or Pentecostal leaning with a theological aversion to suffering. Supporting someone through grief means allowing the grieving individual adequate time and space to process their feelings.

This pastor believes that no charismatic renewal can eliminate human suffering. Those parishioners who hold to the baptism in the Holy Spirit are taught at Saint Luke's United Methodist Church to understand that God is "our refuge and strength...a present help in the time of trouble." Yet, this help does not preclude problems in life. In fact, the presence of the Holy Spirit comforts the believer in trouble. The power of the Spirit remains distinct from magic. Magic attempts to control elements in life. This means having the ability to change adversity in life. This means having the ability to change adversity in life. This means having the ability to change adversity at a whim. The Spirit of God remains less temperamental and patient in its approach to life. Rather than manipulate life events, the assistance of the Holy Spirit helps one face life events and triumph in them. As written in Psalms 25, "The Lord shall teach us in the way that God shall choose." The soverginity of God demands that followers must accept the methods of discipline or teaching that the Lord chooses. There is no sin in trials themselves.

God chooses the means of healing in the life of the Christian. Sometimes the healing will come suddenly, but more often it comes slowly and gradually. Robert Schuller, in his book, *Tough Times Don't Last, But Tough People Do*, speaks of how endurance makes for growth in the inner person. Although most people prefer quick solutions to problems, learning to trust God's timing and deliberation proves a much more valuable asset. Sometimes God heals miraculously and instantaneously. Sometimes God heals through medicine or therapy which demands a greater amount of time and patience. Either method can be effective and neither is less important than the other. When counseling a church member, this pastor asks the member to resist the temptation to presume upon God by dictating the means of relief.

Home visitations remain very helpful in developing pastoral care for the grieving.It provides a type of nourishing which makes the words spoken in church have new meaning. As the old saying goes, "many can talk the talk, but few can walk the walk." Putting Christianity into practice makes it come alive. Home visitations remain one method of putting deeds behind the words spoken in church. Fellowship is helpful under any circumstances.

Unfortunately, often the fellowship comes only when the grief comes. The members of St. Luke's receive encouragement to visit each other on days other than Sunday. Once a month there occurs a Sunday brunch after morning worship service. This event has served the church well. The walls of indifference have come down because of it. Bringing this kind of fellowship into the home helps even more and this pastor makes home visits at every available opportunity.

Home visitations should include the membership of the church and not the pastor alone. Getting the parishioners to visit the grieving lends credibility to the love of the Church and of God.

It is easy for the grieving to think, "Well, of course, the pastor has come, it is her job to do so." But when other parishioners visit, it makes them know that love is the motivation, not duty alone. Some have become active participants through the influence of others, not the pastor. Home visitations have helped tremendously. Hospital and prison visitations are also helpful.

Finally, the ministry of the local church to the grieving should include non-members of the parish. This becomes a tool of evangelism for the church and for the Lord. As often as possible, this pastor extends to friends and acquaintances of a parishioner the benefit of pastoral care. A visit to the grieving member of the congregation is followed by a visit to the object of the grief, i.e., a sick relative, a son in trouble, a husband separated, etc. Sometimes the doors of reception are not open, yet when they are open an evangelistic appeal comes through this method.   Charles R. Swindoll's work, *Improving Your Service: The Art of Unselfish Living*, has helped me attempt an unselfish lifestyle.   In the chapter, *"The Influence of a Servant"*, Swindoll proclaims that Christians "march to a different drummer."   If Christians only help those who help them, what reward do they have? St. Luke's has broadened the definition of grief and therefore we have broadened the scope of our ministry to the grieving.

These supports for ministry to the grieving constitute the pastoral support I utilize at St. Lukes United Methodist Church. Thus far, these methods have worked satisfactorily, yet when a difficult case arises, a referral to a Christian counseling center proves helpful. Also, other types of assistance can lend help. For example, the help line, a crisis line and even referrals for food and financial assistance may provide help. What I pray for now is what Robert Schuller suggests in his book, *Reach Out for New Life,* enthusiasm.   With enthusiasm your "mountains can turn into miracles!" It is my belief that we owe our sisters enthusiastic care and support in their times of grief. For these are opportunities to show love and concern and to even assist in moving mountains.   Grief should be seen as a time for reflection and re-evaluation of one's life.   It can become a healthy, productive time if handled properly.

Bibliography

The Grief Recover Handbook, James and Chevy (Harper and Row).

On Death and Dying, Kubler-Ross.

Questions and Answers on Death and Dying, Kubler-Ross (Collin Books).

When Bad Things Happen to Good People, Kushner, Harold (Avon Books).

Comforting Those Who Grieve--A Guide To Helping Others Doug Manning (Harper and Row).

Don't Take My Grief Away From Me, Doug Manning.

Life After Life, Raymond Moody (Bantam Books).

The Bereaved Parent, Harriett Schiff (Crown Publishers).

Living Through Personal Crisis, Ann Kaiser Stearns (Ballantine Books).

Coming Back: Rebuilding Lives After Crisis and Loss Ann Kaiser Stearns.

Janette Chandler-Kotey, M. Div., Oral Roberts University, currently serves as Senior Pastor of the St. Lukes United Methodist Church in Tulsa, Oklahoma. Completing degree requirements for a Doctorate of Ministries, Janette serves as preacher, praise leader and workshop leader for numerous women's gatherings. An ordained elder in the United Methodist Church, she is married to Raymond Kotey and mother of Lillian NaaDei (Queen), Rita Kouko (Second Daughter), Jennifer Kochoo (Third Daughter).

In Part

Part of me
     just wants to jump up and shout
in that Pentecostal-church-two-step way
with the frenzy of the drum beat yelling
and the organ talking back to
     my moving feet.

Part of me
     just wants to sit down and cry
in that I-got-the-blues-my-feets-is-
tired way
with the scream of the saxophone whining
     and the piano moaning back at
     my wringing hands.

     When the parts of me gets it together I
put on my Sunday-go-to-meeting dress
with a hat tipped
over my eyes singing amazing grace
so's my tired soul can sing and cry/dance and
dirge
     all she wants at the same time.

Valerie J. Bridgeman Davis
July 25, 1991

CHAPTER 8
Releasing Our Womanist Song
Gale Kennebrew Moore

"There's a song inside of me
I can hardly wait to see
What it is I have to say
or the music I will play

It has been so long in coming
First the thought, then some humming
but before I find my key
something stifles it in me
What keeps my song from being sung?
Past hurts, deep fears, a timid tongue?
What threat stands guard before my face?
A tyrant, or demons besieging my space?

Well now its tired of being repressed
It demands to be expressed!
What a shame to keep a song
Cramped in silence oh so long.

"Release your song said the Spirit to me...
You'll never be you till you song is free...
While you debate, decide get ready to sing...
The song could die like a still born thing."

Struck by the peril of further delay
My song like a flood came forcing its way.

Up from within, down from above (And I heard it)
A kingdom built on the power of love
Thank God my song has been set free!
The rhythm and the words are right for me!
I'm finally ready to sing out strong
My soul is saying...this is my song!"
                    (Forbes, 1986)

Releasing the Womanist Song:
Healing The Critical Voice

"The Little Engine That Could"

When I was a child my motto was "I can't".
This motto was given to me by my well meaning and
protective mother.   I was a sensitive child
emotionally and short and petite physically. So when
I attempted to climb the backyard fence like other
children I would hear a voice calling out to
me"...you can't climb up there...you might get hurt!"
Or when I desperately wanted to sing like Diana Ross
of the Supremes I would stand in front of the living
room mirror with a hairbrush handle in my hand
jamming to the tune of "You Can't Hurry Love". In
my minds eye I was on the stage of the Regal Theater
when I would hear my sister's voice saying: "you
can't sing".

My critical voice "I can't" was challenged the
day elementary school teacher decided that my petite
size and quiet personality was exactly what she
needed in the school play: The Little Engine That
Could. I'm sure that she had no idea how selecting
me to play the part of The Little Engine That Could
would change my life and how the process of having
to practice the words: "I think I can, I know I can,
I knew I could"...would change me. As I practiced
these words they became internalized and integrated
as part of my self image. When my critical voice, "I

can't", surfaces, and it still does, especially at the beginning of a particularly difficult task, I do have another voice. I have a voice that says, oh yes you can...remember..."I think can, I know I can, I knew I could." The witness of past experiences of when I could and did succeed and accomplish my goals recites a litany to my spirit and my critical voice is issued a challenge. It is at this point that I choose which voice I will believe, accept and subsequently act on.

Everyone has memories of being told something that they believed and accepted about themselves that was for the most part intended to protect them from hurt, pain or disappointment. This does not negate that some memories may include verbal abuse that was intended to harm. These scripts need to be changed for it does not enhance our sense of well being. I call these critical voices. These also include scripts that were at one time true for us that are now out dated. In my pastoral care experience with women I have heard critical voices such as: "I don't count, I don't deserve to be happy, I am not worthy, I am not capable, and I am not loved".

Critical voices are common place to all of us. As African-American women we have had to overcome a unique set of voices that said we are ugly, wicked, mean, too dark, hair too nappy, funny talking, big nosed, too bossy...etc. I propose that these critical voices are transmitted down through the generations from within our families of origin and from a society and culture that at any given time may decide what is "in" and what is "out".

In this chapter I will show the origin of these critical voice and the process of gaining freedom and healing from the pain of living our life listening, believing and acting as if these critical voices are true when indeed they are not. There is freedom and healing available for us all. The process is not hard but it does take courage. It involves some pain yes, but not as much pain as we are currently experiencing from accepting the inaccuracy of these critical voices. You can stand up and say "no" to the critical voices active in your life and "yes" to the song that lives deep inside of you. The song, your song that lives at the center of your being knows that you are a blessed creation of God. The Blessedness of Creation: It's Origins..."And God stepped out on space and looked around and said: I'm lonely,... (Johnson, 1968:17). God's primary motivation for creating humankind was companionship. I propose that is was only in relationship to another being that God's longing for companionship was met. "And God walked around and looked around at all that...(God) had made...and said: I'm lonely still. Then up from the bank of the river God scooped the clay and toiled over it until (God) created it in (God's) own image and then became a living soul." (Johnson, 1968:19)." It was not in relationship to objects but to persons that God was able to bestow God's image.

Humanity is loved and valued by God. Every person is a beloved creation of God. Humanity is created in the image and likeness of God. According to 1 Corinthians 4:7, God has housed God's spirit (an essence of God's self expression) in our "earthen vessels".

When we were created we received the breath of life which quickened us. God gave humankind an unique gift of creative free will and purpose. Humanity has the innate gift of co-creation which is God's desire to create an expression of God's self through us. It is at this point that we received our "song". James Forbes (1985) speaks of humanity having a song to sing in reference to the process of coming to be and finding one's creative purpose. Coming to sing one's song, as James Forbes describes it, is to find the courage, strength and skill to come forth to do and be what a person believes is God's desire to co-creatively express through them.

I believe that it is human nature to forget that the essence of the spirit that empowers us comes from God. It is also human nature to forget that we have the spirit of God within us. African-American women struggle with that fact that we have "treasures in these earthen vessels. (1 Corinthians 4:7)" Either extreme is problematic in our relationships with ourselves, others and God.

In my theology, when we listen to our critical voices we have a distorted understanding of our purpose and meaning of our existence. The spirit of God within us motivates us to seek harmony with ourselves. The sole purpose of critical voices is to maintain our current state of distorted understanding, purpose and existence. The process of releasing our womanist song is a struggle between the spirit of God within us striving for harmony and our critical voices that seek to maintain our current state of distorted understanding. We are in a condition of human existence that denies the integration of spirit housed in clay.

Healing occurs as we realize, verbalize (to ourselves, others and God) our critical voices, beliefs and actions that maintain our painful existence and keep us from releasing our womanist song. Our creative awareness is refocused and we risk releasing our womanist song by believing and subsequently acting upon the voice of God within us that believes and knows that we are beloved and valued creations of God given the gift of co-creation.

Through the model of Jesus the Incarnate Christ we are shown the appropriate responses to every critical voice. Through the Holy Spirit we are given a new song that contradicts every critical voice intrapersonally and interpersonally. "Fellowshipping with God is the beginning and end of human liberation. The liberated person is the one who encounters God in faith, that is, in conviction and trust that one's true humanity is actualized in God...This vertical dimension of faith is the essential response to the gospel and is thus the heart of liberation's meaning from the human side. This is why conversion, prayer, and community worship are dominant motifs in the black religion when the people testify that they met Jesus "early one Thursday morning"...They are talking about the importance of the divine encounter."

Singing our womanist song begins with using whatever ingredients we have as women. I learned an example of this as a child. My mother was a beautician. I recall watching her with her clients. When a client would come into the shop looking for a "new" or "refreshed" style, before my mother began she would study the client's hair: its texture, shape, color, condition, length. My mother would then consider the client's preferences and what she knew of their personality. Of course other factors influenced the final outcome such as: how much time was available, my mother's energy level, was this person a particularly difficult client, a scheduled appointment, etc. This was part of the preparation aspect of creating or re-creating order, beauty and form out of an unstylish, weather worn head of hair.

In supervision of students in Clinical Pastoral Education and as a womanist I am reminded that all women are blessed creations and co-creators. I am a lump of clay, shaped in God's own image and empowered by God's spirit. As lumps of clay we are shaped in certain ways, we come in different, brokenness and wholeness as a way to establish, maintain and when the time comes, end relationships.

My supervisory style is cooperative. I believe I am a singing coach for other women who are in the process of learning to release their womanist song. At the same time I am constantly updating and revising my song. Having an awareness of my own clayness helps me to discern, work with and wait patiently for the shape, form, substance, texture, that each woman will project. Having an awareness of God's Spirit within me helps me to recognize and value the Spirit of God within others. Singing my song helps me to model the integration of Spirit housed in clay with other women and become their singing coach. I firmly believe that releasing one's womanist song will occur if there exists an affirming, nurturing and challenging learning environment. For me the African-American religious experience along with Clinical Pastoral Education has been this learning environment.

It is my desire to help students come to know and sing their song in the beauty and fullness of the power of God. Three ingredients are necessary for this. I have used Letty Russell's definition of the process whereby persons come to true humanity as a model and propose the following:
(1) students must come to understand and remember their past, and utilize this awareness in the shaping of their present world and relationships and future; (2) have a community of faith which nurtures, supports and challenges when whereby they discover themselves; (3) experience acceptance by God, themselves and others.

Human beings are relational: in relationship with family, themselves, culture, and institutions. From the beginning of life the unborn fetus is connected to its mother who provides all of the nutrients and the environment necessary for its development. Every human being begins life's journey this way, connected in relationship. The need for relationships continues in social forms throughout life. It is the natural striving of humanity to live in groups and form and develop meaningful, deep and consistent relationships among its members.

Just as humanity came into being as a result of God breathing God's spirit into humanity's nostrils the human personality does not come into being until it receives the "breath" of interaction with another human being. The human personality is formed, created and developed out of interpersonal relationships. Harry stack Sullivan asserts that the mind and the psychic structures that comprise it evolve out of human interactions. Our relationships may be internal, external, fantasied or real but they essentially center ·around interactions with other humans.

We need to change responses that have been formed by prior relationships into workable, adaptive identities that function to enhance our sense of self is comparable to the meaning of Jesus Christ taking on the body of humankind to redeem humanity. The universal nature of goodness/badness is akin to the universal nature of sin. Originally, all persons were created good and blessed. However, we are born into a world where perfection does not exist and hence we learn that we too are not perfect. A world that is wounded where we are wounded.

Understanding my own personal history has greatly informed my work as a Supervisor in Training with the Association of Clinical Pastoral Education, Inc. I began with my own awareness of my humanness and woundedness. As an African-American female, I have struggled with issues of believing that I am bad because of the color of my skin and texture of my hair. As an adult child of an alcoholic father I have struggled with trust, intimacy, nurturing, and self esteem. The resolution of these issues was a process which was painful. However, in the process there had been relationships that enabled me to believe in the goodness within me, in others and, the world, in spite of my pain. Understanding this has helped me claim those areas in my past that are my strength and work with them in my supervisory relationships and let go of those that hinder me.

Clinical Pastoral Education residency training was conducted in a primarily all white, suburban hospital where I was the first African-American student to enroll in a unit of CPE. My supervisor was a white, middle class, conservative, male and my group was primarily all white male with one other white female. My supervisor was assertive and confrontational.

During my residency my supervisor was split between good supervisor/bad supervisor. As I related to the good supervisor I projected dependency. My relational stance was helpless and I communicated that I couldn't survive and wanted him to take care of me. My previous history had experiences where white male teachers felt sorry for me and didn't expect much from me. These were the "good" white folks. However, when my supervisor wisely and quite honestly did not respond to me in this manner I labeled him "bad" supervisor. This is when my learning occurred.

I had an experience as a child with a white owner of a local store. Because of my supervisor's non caretaking role, and a small resemblance he had to this store owner I relived the anger and humiliation I experienced when I was thrown out of the school store in front of my classmates for using profane language. From that experience I concluded that I would not be accepted by white people if I was my spontaneous self. In fact, I would be rejected. During the first two quarters of my training, I presented a nice, personable persona. I was complimentary to staff, patients, peers and somewhat distant toward my supervisor. My nickname was "sweet tooth." As the unit progressed and "sweet tooth's" energy level waned and as my supervisor began confronting my passive aggressive behavior such as tardiness and not turning in my written assignments in a timely manner, I began to express my spontaneity and real feelings and became more a part of the group. To my surprise when I began to be authentic, I was more accepted than when I was hidden and withholding. The group trusted me more and valued the insight and perspective I shared. Instead of being rejected I was accepted in the fullness of my divinity and humanity, i.e., good enough self image.

I use projective identifications to diagnose the area of relationship and sense of self that is hurting with students. I call attention to the identification as a means of confronting the image of the self that is seeking balance and integration. I facilitate reflection with the student about the effects of their projective identification on others and help them explore other ways they can enhance their life.

I also utilized aspects of object relations theory

during a recent woman's conference. Our group consisted of five women and two facilitators. I began the group reciting James Forbes poem "Release Your Song" which set the tone for the rest of the workshop. Each of us began telling our stories. Karen was a health care worker in her mid thirties and admits she played the caretaker role in her relationships most of her life. She had experienced burnout and had been battling for her mental health since last year. Karen was in touch with a part of herself that she never wanted to listen to before who would no longer be denied. She was aware of a strong critical voice that said "I can't dream because my dreams never come true". Because of this critical voice she was afraid to get in touch with her inner self where her dreams lived. Initially, Karen didn't feel she could have what she wanted so she was depressed most of the time to the point that everyday was a struggle for her. I talked about naming, claiming and choosing in reference to our critical voice. I suggested that we each write what our critical voice was saying to us on paper and share them with each other. As we shared we listened, cared for and gave attention to the pain in our lives as a result of listening to and believing in the power these critical voices had in our lives. We each shared our stories and the grip that these critical voices had on each of us. Right there in the group these critical voices were challenged as I along with the other facilitator shared how we were experiencing each member of the group. We spoke words that contradicted the potency of the critical voices and the other members of the group supported our observations. We brought the session to a close by singing "A Fresh Word and a New Song" together. I read the entire 8th chapter of Romans to the group reading "critical voice" in the place where "flesh" is written. We took the paper with our critical voice written on it and burned it while singing "A Fresh Word and a New Song". Karen did indeed release her womanist song with the part of herself that could dream and sing and dance. We touched on the tender spots in all of us and as one member wrote these spots need to be exposed to the light of day for healing to begin. The critical voices lose their power when brought to the light of day and the group experience was a powerful healing tool.

Releasing our womanist song is a process. Initially as African-American women we begin the journey making sure that we are as acceptable as we believed we should be. We did internalize characteristics that have enabled us to survive. These patterns are well developed and readjusting those behaviors that do not enhance our relationships is a struggle. Some women begin re-writing their "bad me" song by finding a comfortable "key". What is important is to begin the process of change by overcoming the anxiety and internal oppression of our critical voices and begin the discovering and singing our womanist song. Change and learning to release our womanist song occurs as we enter into an experience/interaction, reflection, documentation, sharing and feedback process.

EXPERIENCE/INTERACTION:

Learning begins with an experience or interaction. This can be a personal experience as defined as one that does not initially involve direct interaction with another person. Or the experience can be an interaction that directly involves another person. In order for learning to occur there must be an experience or interaction between us and object. Object in this sense does not necessarily have to be human, for example, the experience can be with nature, an aspect of ourself through a dream, reading a book, with God through prayer or meditation. Ideally, we begin with a non-human object then an interaction with a human will occur at some point. The experience or interaction will be significant enough to motivate us to the next stage reflection.

REFLECTION:

This is the stage where we think and feel intentionally about the experience or interaction. We search for meaning or the unveiling of the reality inherent in the first stage. This is the stage where we relive, reconsider, review, turn and examine the experience in as many aspects as possible. The fetus is developing. Our womanist song is being formulated and possible musical notes and meters are being examined. It should be noted that in this stage we utilize both cognitive and affective resources that are available to use and search for integration of the two. Dialogue in this stage can be internal within self or external with another person. Toward the end of this stage there is a restlessness that is the labor period of the third stage documentation.

DOCUMENTATION:

This is the birthday stage. Learning is solidified. There is evidence of learning/change in a concrete, manifested form that is communicated through dialogue. Visually learning can be communicated in creative artistic expression, dance, the written word, or changes in behavior. Audibly learning can. be demonstrated in the spoken word, through song, music. Learning can also be documented through touch and body language, cognitively though changes in attitudes and thinking and affectively through new feelings and subsequent actions.

SHARING AND FEEDBACK:

Sharing and feedback enhances our learning by making it an open ended. Openness to feedback, critique and evaluation involves risk yet it enables us to start the learning cycle again by re-integrating the new knowledge and experience that resulted from feedback from our community. Sharing and feedback is the giving and receiving dimension of learning, where we share what we have learned with our community of sisters and invite them to begin the learning process in order to release their womanist song.

Endnotes

[1] James Forbes, *Release Your Song,* excerpts read by author, Lyman Beecher Lecture Series. Cassette #3. Yale Divinity School, 1986.

[2] James Weldon Johnson, *The Creation*, God's Trombones, (New York: Viking Press, 1968), p. 17.

[3] Ibid, p. 19

[4] II Corinthians 4:7

[5] James Forbes, *Release Your Song,* excerpts read by author, Lyman Beecher Lecture Series. Cassette #3. Yale Divinity School, 1885.

[6] II Corinthians 4:7.

[7] James Cone, *God of the Oppressed,* (New York: Seabury Press, 1975), p. 141.

[8] Genesis 3:5

[9] Sheldon Cashdan, *Object Relations Therapy*, (New York: W. W. Norton, 1988), p. 52.

[10] Ibid., p. 44.

[11] Ibid, p. 77.

Bibliography

Cannon, Katie G. *Black Womanist Ethics*. Atlanta: Scholars Press, 1988.

Forbes, James *Release Your Song*. Excepts read by the author.

Lyman Beecher Lecture Series. Cassette #3. Yale Divinity School, 1985.

Fox, Matthew. A *Spirituality Named Compassion and the Healing of the Global Village, Humpty Dumpty and Us*. Minneapolis: Winston Press, Inc., 1979.

Grant, Jacquelyn. *White Women's Christ and Black Women's Jesus*. Atlanta: Scholars Press, 1989.

Johnson, James Weldon. *God's Trombones*. New York: Viking Press 1968.

Russell, Letty. *Human Liberation in a Feminist Perspective - A Theology*. Westminister Press, 1974.
Tillich, Paul. *The Courage To Be*. New Haven: Yale University Press, 1952.

Augsburger, David. *Caring Enough to Confront.* Ventura, CA, Regal Books, 1981. Freire, Paulo. *Pedagogy of the Oppressed.* New York: Continuum Publishing Corp., 1970.

Joyce, Bruce and Weil, Marsh. *Models of Teaching, Third Edition.* Englewood Cliffs: Prentice Hall, 1980.

Larse, Earnie. *Old Patterns New Truths.* Minneapolis: Hazelden, 1988.

Lissick, Shelia Bayle and Jahns, Elise Marquam. *Creating Choices.* Minneapolis: Hazelden, 1990.

Yalom, Irvin. *The Theory and Practice of Group Psychtheraphy. Third Edition. 3* New York: Basic Books, Inc., 1985.

Anderson, Herbert and Mitchell, Kenneth. *All Our Losses, All Our Griefs.* Philadelphia: Westminster Press, 1983.

Bowlby, John. *Attachment.* New York: Basic Books, Inc., 1969.

Bowlby, John. *Separation Anxiety and Anger.* New York: Basic Books, Inc., 1973.

Cashdan, Sheldon. *Object Relations Therapy.* New York: W.W. Norton & Company, Inc., 1988.

Gerkin, Charles V. *The Living Human Document.* Nashville: Abingdon, 1984.

Sullivan, Harry Stack. *The Interpersonal Theory of Psychiatry.* Edited by Helen Swick Perry and Mary Ladd Gawell, with an introduction by Mable Blake Cohen. New York: W.W. Norton & Company, Inc., 1953.

Whitfield, Charles L. *Healing the Child Within.* Deerfield Beach, Florida: Health Communications, Inc., 1984.

Gale Kennebrew Moore, M. Div., Chicago
Theological Seminary, met a committee this year for
certification as Associate Supervisor in the
Association for Clinical Pastoral Educators. She
presently serves as Staff Chaplain at the South
Chicago Community Hospital in Chicago, Illinois,
and is a fellow in the College of Chaplains. As
ordained Baptist pastor, Gale preachers, does
workshops, seminars and small groups. She is the
mother of three children, Michael, Angela and
Matthew.

Ode to Black Women

They say,
        we,
        -- black women that we are --
that we hate, distrust, despise each other
that we look for ways to destroy each other
        maybe because of what we've got and want to
keep
        or what we don't have and want to get but,
                -- along with all those other myths about
us --
sensuous, sex-satiated, domineering BLACK women,
        they say we hate each other.
Then......
        I met you and realized
They lied.

                Valerie J. Bridgeman Davis
                1982

CHAPTER 9

"Women's Friendships: Reality and Hope"
Valerie J. Bridgeman Davis

It was a warm Texas evening, even for October 30, 1990. I had gathered ten women who were and are influential in my life. The Event was dubbed my "Sister-Friend Party." Having finished seminary in May, I had launched into an intense self-discovery time with the help of a good counselor. The emotional work was hard as I struggled with painful childhood memories. I was tired. My friend, Emily Hassler, a white woman, suggested a party. Betty Smith, one of my best friends, a black woman, offered to help foot the bill.

The color for the evening was purple, my favorite. I bought sampler items such as baby lotion and perfume, which I arranged in a basket from which each woman chose. Streamers and banners were posted. Each woman was instructed to bring her favorite writing. Emily brought candles which we lit to celebrate mothers/sisters/brothers/fathers lovers/friends in our lives.

We ate pizza and laughed much. We heard each other's desire's, then I prayed for each woman's dreams. It was a powerful gathering of a strange mix of women, black and white, ultra liberal to ultra conservative. One friend shook her head in amazement, "Just think, they all came because you invited them."

With privilege, I told each woman how special she was to me. I thanked God for each of their wisdom, loyalty and power. My regret was that my best friend of ten years, Seleta Metoyer, was unable to come. This party reminded me of all the women who surround, nurture, sustain and love me. It was a long way from 1984, when after three years in San Antonia, Texas, I realized that my life was barren of women friends. Yes, I had Seleta, whom I still cherish, but I felt poor. I was not keeping in touch with friends I had left in Alabama, and I had not ventured beyond my local congregation into San Antonio.

I was lonely, and missing my mother. Growing up, I mostly depended on my sisters and my cousins to be my friend-reflectors, with smatterings of friends here and there. But now, in 1984, I was lonely, scared and unhappy. Instinctively I knew that I had to find women friends, or go crazy. I still remember what I prayed: "God, I need women in my life, to keep me stable, sane. Do something!" The floodgates opened. As editor of the university news service, I did a story on a local clergywoman. Claudette Copeland became the first of the parade of sister/mother/friends that began and continues to enter my life. Women friends have become my mainstay. All of them, but especially my black sisters, have been my "emotional guardians." (Randolph, 1990: 38)."I do not want to minimize the role of all my women friends, but my task at present is to look at the role of black women to black women friendships.

182

Perhaps the most celebrated friendship between women in recent years is that of talk-show host Oprah Winfrey and Gayle King Bumpus, news anchor in Hartford, Conn. A July, 1990 article in Ebony, lifts up their alliance to say "black women have always been a bedrock of stability in each other's lives. (Randolph, 1990:38)." Their relationship is special, containing monetary elements on a much larger scale than most. A generous friend, Winfrey insists money is not an issue. What she gives financially is overshadowed by the emotional support and honesty the two friends share. Winfrey knows, she says, "Gayle would tell her the truth, no matter how painful it was to hear (Randoph, 1990:36)".

The Ebony article is about networking among celebrities. In reality, the article is about black women doing what we do best for one another: caring for one another's souls. Networking is the natural-by-product of good friendships. What do friendships among black women mean in a caring context? How do black women tend one another, and how does this tending lead to wholeness, growth and fulfillment? My task, as I understand it, is to reflect on the real nature and the hope of black women's friendships among themselves as a pastoral care tool.

I do not think there is a monolithic quality among black women's friendships with each other. Indeed, the indication is black women's friendships come in great variety. As I have thought about the pastoral nature of black women's friendships, however, I have come to believe there are some

183

"samenesses" among women who dare to care for one another in significant ways.

What is a friend? The term may mean someone we know only in a club activity, or it may mean someone who will drop everything to respond to your cry of distress. Friendship is chiefly an egalitarian affair. While roles among friends may resemble mother-daughter, pastor-parishioner, lover-lover,teacher-student relationships, the underlying ethos for friendship is the relationship of equals. Each friend. carries an equal degree of responsibility for the growth and continuation of the relationship. Such relationships are formed out of desire, rather than obligation.

Friends are "chosen intimates(Sanford, Donovan, 1985:105)."Friends are people we like, although sometimes for unclear reasons. Friends are additives in our lives. "(They) choose to do what kin are obliged to do. We expect provision from our family. With friends, the basis of the relationship is freedom. Sallie McFague in *Models of God*, notes that freedom is part of the power of friendship: "all other relationships are ringed with duty or utility or desire. Friendship, too, is pregnant with these qualities, but the starting point is delight. For women, and perhaps black women in particular, delight in finding a like soul quickly moves to usefulness. We need someone to run with us. We may be from"a long line of black and going on women (Clifton, 1982:156)" but we rarely run alone. Black women are too familiar with the pain of separation and loneliness. What started in slavery with forced loss now continues in the mobility of our societies. Friends help hold off isolation as they are women who decide to care passionately about the quality of another woman's life, to respect each other's choices, and to allow for each other's differences.

We make friends with people who interest us. We meet them at the laundry mat or church, at work or at school. We make friends with people who share our common goals or needs, with people who are "in the same boat" as we are. Judith Viorst refers to friends of common goals as "special-interest friends (Viorst 1986:1987). Sometimes, we make friends with people very different from us, "a friend who mirrors our fantasies, dreams of a self we wish we could be(Hunt, 1991:81).

But once the bond of friendship is established, the responsibility and expectations begin to be negotiated. Eva Margolies, in *The Best of Friends, the Worst of Enemies*, believes women's friendships are deeply imbedded in their relationship with their mothers. That is, women try to relive or redeem their relationship with mother. Margolies (1985:38) notes that "friends are replacements for the mothers we (women) just left". Her book works out this premise with such issues as intimacy, jealousy, and confidentiality. I agree that women learn at their mother's breast to love/hate and trust/distrust other women. The intensity in which a woman once related to her mother often is played out in her friendships. Mothers fail us, even while trying to support us. And sometimes mothers are just not good at mothering. Mary Wise in her chapter of this work takes up the blessings and bonds of mother and daughter relations.

This search for another parent may cost friends for the woman who cannot identify her needs. "If a woman is searching for monolithic parent substitutes to fulfill needs left over from childhood, her relationships are bound to constantly disappoint her. Surrogate parenting is an unfair request: Who would want the time-consuming responsibility of raising another adult "(Sanford, Donovan, 1985:38)? And yet, I think Black women often do "raise each other," alternating between roles of mother, sister, soulmate.

Among black women this tendency may be heightened by the tradition of "Big Mamas." Big mamas are not only one's blood grand-and great grandmothers, but also other women who have earned a place in the family. My own big mamas included my maternal and paternal grandmothers, a girlfriend's mother, Bobbie Reynold's and the neighbor up the hill, Mrs. Essie Pope. I learned to cook, can vegetables and do home remedies from my mother and my grandmothers. I heard I was a wonderful child from Bobbie. I learned to make teacakes and appreciate my upbringing from Mrs Essie. In fact, my early images of God are rooted in the old women, and the ones who joined them for quilting bees and canning excursions. As I listen to other black women, the "nuclear" family included women and men whom the dominate culture would refer to as extended family, or less, "just friends."

For black women, these "play" big mamas are

a real, essential part of our lives. Older friends become echoes of the wisdom and support of these big mamas. Black life seems very clearly organized around a clan model of wise men and women, story tellers, chieftains and such. What may appear enmeshment in the dominate culture is an attempt to be faithful to the system among blacks. Black women have been taught to hang in with each other no matter what. Such loyalty can be healthy, or it can be sick dependency on a person or persons who should long have been cut from one's life. I will return to this idea later.

So friends come from every direction. The most unlikely combinations will be best of friends. People cross generational, class and race lines to find someone who sees them for who they are and loves them nonetheless. Who can fathom why an old woman missionary and a young female rap artist might be friends? One provides continuity to life, with a wealth of experience and memories. The other adds spice and rhythm. They do not bring the same thing, but they bring the same commitment and they like each other.

Life transitions will often bring new friends and lead us to let go of others. My friend, Daisy Thomas Quinney, refers to this happening as "God giving us friends for a season and a reason." In the book, *Necessary Losses*, Judith Viorst refers to the same process as historical friends who have been with us since when, and crossroads friends we meet in the transition. Marjory Zoet Bankston, in her book, *Seasons of Friendships*, describes life's empty friendship's as seasonal, sometimes including the same person in each season as in the story of Ruth and Naomi, but more often needing different people for each season. For instance, the woman who went through high school acne with you may drop out of your life by the time you are finished college.

This is not always the case, but few of us have many friends from the past. I remember, painfully, the day that my best friend from elementary school, Sabrina Reynolds, and I realized that we no longer had anything in common. It was the year The Color Purple was playing in movie theaters throughout the country. I had read the book three or four times. When I went home to Alabama, Sabrina and I did the usual ritual, asking about each other's family. There was an uncomfortable pause. Fishing for a common topic, I asked if she had seen the movie. She had not heard of it. We looked at each other and acknowledged we had grown in different directions. I felt I had lost a part of me. Sabrina's family had been my second home growing up. I still make an effort to see her and her family whenever I am in Alabama. We are historical friends, and care very much about one another, but I don't image that we will call each other at 3 o' clock in the morning.

Of course, there are plenty of friendships that have lasted more than twenty years. My mother and her best friend have maintained strong ties living miles apart with the aid of the telephone, writing and occasional visits. Their relationship fall in the category of "for life" friends, "a commitment that grows and develops out of the relationship itself, out of a friendship that withstands the test of time, of separation, of togetherness, of uneven levels of development, of uncertain steps toward change, of growth that crawls one moment and gallops the next." (Rubin, 1985: 91).

The grounding for friendships, for me, is the pastoral nature they take on. Friends know they are watching for one another's very life. I believe there is a God-like quality in friendships. Proverbs 18:24 speaks of a friend who sticks closer than a brother or sister. In the black church tradition, this friend is most always interpreted as Jesus. This text is often linked with Matthew 11:19, where Jesus is called a friend of tax collectors and sinners. In addition, Jesus called his disciples friends, changing for eternity the inferior-superior nature of the relationship. Yes, Jesus is our savior and redeemer, but he chooses to befriend us, giving us opportunity for responsibility and reciprocity.

I am always struck by the number of songs declaring "there's no friend like Jesus," or "what a friend we have in Jesus." These songs are in keeping with biblical and black tradition. But during the 1991 Woman to Woman Ministries Advance, I got a clearer vision of how friendship with Jesus works among black women. We cried and sang, "there's not a friend like the lowly Jesus," while we clung to each other. Intuitively we know we meet the Savior's care in each other's arms. We know God knows all our pain, but we wrestle with God in the presence of friends. To be isolated is to be sick. Friends help with the friendship of Jesus keep us sane. In the poem, "In Answer to the Question: Have you Ever Considered Suicide," Kate Rushin instructs her "gurl" friend:

> If you ever hear me
> Talkin bout killin my frail self
> Come and get me
> Sit with me until that spell passes
> (Rushin, 1990:3)

To sit with a friend is to participate in the black church tradition's idea of rocking someone's soul in the bosom of Abraham, or sitting their body in the lap of Jesus.

In *Models of God*, McFague (1987:, 60) points out that friendship with Jesus and God is a frequent metaphor among the mystics. McFaque says "to be friends with God is the most astounding possibility, for whereas a mother desires your existence and a lover finds you valuable, a friend likes you." Befriending is God's way of relating. Among black women, being liked is a high priority commodity. Black women have too often been the target of intense hatred and disdain. To know that God not only loves us but likes us is good news.

I believe God ordains friendships among humans to mirror God's own care for us. When the words were uttered, "it is not good for the human to be alone," the life-carrying human was brought forth to affirm that it need never be so again. We often are struck with the male-female quality of creation. I am stuck with the relational quality. We need each other. The preacher of Ecclesiastes says in 4:9-12, that when two are together they may get a good return on their involvement, they lift one another up and keep each other warm. If the numbers increase by only one, the bond is hard to break.

In American society, the "significant other" is valued, but Mary Hunt (1991:38) notes in *Fierece Tenderness*, women have often worked under the principle of the writer of Ecclesiastes, preferring a "significant multitude." Dee Brestin (1988:36) calls this tendency "the web of relationships." This principle seems to resonate among black women. For black women, friendship is primarily systemic, not singular, encompassing a network in which each strand of the web is connected. We may not know each of our friends, but we are affected by them. When a loss-producing power imposes on the web, the pain reverberates through the whole system. We cry when our friends lose friends, wailing against the loss that is like our own. The friend's momentary diminishing diminishes us. Our heart breaks in response. One of the sister-friends in our congregation, Dyna Cole, calls this "loving the people who love the people you love."

From this point, I will address how we make and keep the friends we have, what may we reasonably expect and how we let go of damaging relationships.
I have noticed a pattern among my own friendships which I have heard echoed from other women. The three words I have chosen with which to address this pattern are: attending, intending and contending.

191

Friendships never occur until we pay attention to another person. The tendency to walk past others without acknowledging them is great in a society where the highest value is the one. Yet in order to even consider a relationship, we must give purposeful pause. This attending is what Brestin (1988:35) calls recognition. We must catch another's eye or listen carefully to their voice. One way attending happens among women is in the surge of women's retreats and conferences that provide intimacy among strangers. In these settings, women recognize that "there are certain things about being a woman that only another woman can understand (Margolies, 1985:89)." This is the story-telling stage. Women give each other space to share history. Among black women, the sharing often is around the anger of being excluded by the larger society, and abused by those in our community men and women who are trapped in their own pain.

This attending stage may have intimate moments, but not an intimate relationship. This period is guarded and tentative. It is in this time that women decide whether or not they will bestow the title "friend." People rarely plunge in and stay at a deep level while attending. Even at conferences where intimacy may be intense, women do not leave believing all two hundred women present are their friends. During the time a woman is being attended, she is blessed with the realization that someone acknowledges her existence. It is the call into relationship which says, "I see you standing there, I recognize your pain and your potential." Many black women are accustomed to being dismissed or ignored. But when another woman stops to say, "yes I see you," affirmation occurs. One has been noticed and encouraged, but not necessarily befriended. Yet, this may be like what Bankston means by "summer friends" as one who "connects deeply and then slips out of our lives because they are not rooted in an on-going community."

Attending to another's presence opens the possibility of traveling together, of becoming friends. The risen Savior got the attention of two disciples on the trip to Emmaus as he interrupted their lives and attended their questions. During the time of attending, choosing occurs and gives way to intentionally signing on to another's life for a longer season than an hour.

Intending is, as I understand it, the next step in the development of friendship. Once we have given our attention to another, we moved toward intentionality. On the road to Emmaus, intending occurs when the disciples asked Jesus to abide with them. Intending is abiding, remaining for the intricate parts of another that can not be found out merely in story-telling time. It is the time of the shared meal. We begin to negotiate the streams of the relationship, deciding together what shape the relationship will take. The bond is strengthened as friends weave into each other's lives, all the while determining what is too close, what is enough. We began to make a conscious decision"to make a commitment to friendship without knowing where it will lead (Bankston, 1987:14)".

Black women have historically started the process of intending in the kitchen. I have an original painting by San Antonio artist Carolyn Thomas of two black women sitting over coffee, titled "This is Me, Girl." The painting demonstrates two friends who have carved out time in their lives in which to expose the real person to each other. This takes time, space and energy. It is the time in which we begin to develop"a language of love so the relationship can thrive over time and in memory (Bankston, 1987:45)" The black community struggles with sexuality as does the larger society, and black women are no exception. Among black women there seems to be an ease in which intending includes playing together, gift-giving, caressing, and hugging. The ease continues in the sharing of stories and telling the truth. We do the stuff of friendship, reminding our friend and ourselves how much we love them. Thus, "friendships need reverence, candor, space, and specificity. Most of all they require some sort of periodic celebration to renew and refresh the bonds in a community of friends (Hunt, 1991: 117)."

Intending includes bodily care. I enjoy the tactile and sensual quality of my relationship with a friend, Betty, who gives me a message as a gift each week "because you need it and so do I". I am nourished by her touch which communicates her prayers for me. Intending is handling with care. I"ve known of women who examined one another's bodies for signs of cancer or other distress. The checking comes with such words as: "Girl, this mole has changed. You better get this checked. Don't you go dying on me."

Intending is where the current runs both ways. Not only do we reflect the friend, we learn about ourselves. "Friends become for us a mirror on the self; and what we see there, whether it pleasures or pains us, helps to affirm those parts of self we like and respect and to change those whose reflection brings us discomfort (Hunt, 1991:81)."

Both attending and intending leads to contending for the right of the friend to grow and develop. During this time, friends push one another away from the comfort zones of their lives. For me, it seemed that all my friends began about the same time to say to me, "when are you going to do something about your writing.." I had talked, for years about being a writer, but I was not writing.." Now in the shadow of these women who have contended for my gifts, not allowing even me to ignore or minimize them, I am writing. Mary Hunt identifies this as a common seam in the fabric of women's friendships, what she calls"the muse-like women friends who call forth truths and talents that might have been left hidden without their beckon. (Hunt, 1991:151)."

Contending is interceding. Black women have interceded for each other for years. There are stories, sure of tension among "field hands" and "house niggers," but even in that horrific culture, the women banded together to save as many lives as possible. Among black women, and especially church women, prayer intercession is a major form of contending. This contending leads women to actively and passionately carry each other's concerns to God and in their own hearts. It leads women to look for jobs and baby-sitters for one another. Intercession is what Oprah Winfrey did when she hired a nanny for her best friend so she would not have to interrupt her career(Randolph: 1990:38).

I have written with enthusiasm about the joys of black women's friendships. They come in variety, nourish us at our roots, and push us on to wholeness. We must pay attention to one another, that we intend the best of each other and that we contend for one another's dreams and development. I have sang the praise of womanist care. There is much more that could be said. When I use the term "stage", I do not mean to suggest that the doing of friendship is linear. Rather, at any time in any relationship, the pattern may move from attending to contending, back to intending. I may be more inclined to say intending is the vessel which encases the relationship and allows for the attending and contending that occurs within.

Black women's friendships are not without pain or disappointment, or sometimes destruction. One may not write of black women's friendships without looking, if only briefly, at the underside. As with faith, so friendship cannot be proven unless it is tested. We often speak of "fair-weather"friends, but the storms must rise before we may know that some people will not hang in the hard times. Sometimes, the friendships which so potently heal are the same ones that crush us, leaving us feeling defenseless.

"That's because the only people who can hurt us are the ones we really care about," one woman friend said. One of the primary ways women hurt one another is betrayal. "The sin against the friend is betrayal... The betrayer is the one who acts the friend" but opens the door from within to the enemy. (Mcfague, 1987:162)." To betray a friend is to expose her to people who do not like her who wish her ill, with no protection. This is treacherous and damning.

Betrayal may come in many forms. One of the most prevalent is the one reflected in Proverbs 16:28: "a whisperer separates close friends." Because of the tendency toward group friendships, the chance of sharing information not for general consumption is great. Black women are no different. Sometimes, the group dynamics finds the friend in the position of "double-dealing," appeasing one friend at the sake of another, while saying something different when in the presence of the original friend. "The fact is that betrayal, deception, duplicity, competition and jealousy are all real human emotions and behaviors in which real people engage. Women friends, sadly, are no different (Hunt, 1991:39)."

Aside from the ever-present issue of gossip, communication betrayal may be even more subtle. Women's friendships in general often operate under the credo of "because you're a woman you should instinctively know what I need. (Margolies, 1985:283)." This can cause confusion, anger and hurt when a friend is unable to discern another's needs because she has not been explicitly told. The result is that the injured friend will often sulk, be vindictive or let the offenses accumulate without the friend knowing she has offended. The problem is, our unconscious does not often let us get away with repression. As my mother, Bernice Bridgeman, says, "if it doesn't come out straight, it'll come out crooked." We may believe that we are being straight and open, but in fact may be hiding our feelings, even from ourselves. We cannot assume that our sister-friends understand our wants or needs. We must be willing to effectively communicate them. Black women seem especially susceptible to the myth of the all-knowing friend. Because of the meta-history black women share, we often forget that, while we do share common history, our lives are colored greatly by such things as where we grew up, where or if we attended school, and our spiritual journey.

Another issue that arises in women's friendships is the expectation that the friend will always be available. I seem to experience this more heavily among my black women friends than I do among any other group of friends.

I have faced the fury of a friend who felt I did not give all that was demanded. I have felt the guilt of feeling I "should have been there, " when I could not. In the words of Viorst (1986:87), "even the best of friends are friends in spots." No one is able to be ever-present or all things to any one person. This dynamic often gets played out in the church as clergy women struggle to maintain an identity as minister, while having friends. Often in black congregations, women in the church feel that the pastor (female) or the male pastor's wife should befriend every woman in the church merely because she is a woman. This expectation is too great.

The other side of expecting too much is expecting too little. When we're injured, we often push people away who would "be there" for us. The friendship suffers when we are unable to allow the friend to befriend us. For black women who live in the shadow of the "strong, black woman," this is tempting. We labor believing we ought to be able to handle it, and are angry when people allow us to live with the delusion.

"Perhaps the greatest barrier to bonding is low self-esteem itself (Sanford, Donovan, 1985:123)" A woman with low self-esteem fights her own feelings of inadequacy and must work not to project her neediness so strongly into her friendships. "There is probably no quicker way to stagnate or eventually destroy a relationship than to blame another person for our...unhappiness or to expect them to make it all better." It takes a lot of internal strength to feel good about ourselves. Often we depend on others to reflect a "good me" to us. When the friendship is expected to carry the weight of the friend's lack of faith in herself, it suffers and may need to be severed.

Friendships often are endangered when power differences are evident. "Friendship often comes to an abrupt halt when power differences go unrecognized, unchallenged and finally unchanged. (Hunt, 1991: 102)." I was very aware of my own feelings of jealousy and of being left out as a friend moved on to a higher, more prestigious job. And I have been stung by the cattiness of a friend who begrudged my place in a seminar she wanted to lead. Sometimes the imbalance is caused by the inability to meet needs. When one friend can provide monetarily and the other cannot reciprocate, the relationship is uneven unless there is another commodity that the other provides. Power struggles happen when we feel threatened by the success, beauty or influence of friends. Women first must be willing to admit when one person owns more power before they can negotiate how the relationship will fare. Because black women have been trained to view, to some extent, all sister-friend relationship as equal, we sometimes lie to ourselves about the fact that we rank our friends. Coming clean and clear helps eliminate the power struggle.

Gossip, inaccurate or muddled communication, unhealthy expectations, low self-esteem and unequal power are hindrances in any relationship. Among black women they are grist for a larger hurt, the hurt of being "rejected by your own." Because black people tend to think communally, any betrayal carries shattering power. But we black women know we need each other, so we often try to work through betrayal to reconciliation. When done correctly, this includes telling the friend how you feel about being betrayed; allowing the friend to make restitution; then, renegotiating the boundaries of the relationship. This is how friendship is tempered.

Not all friendships should be reconciled. Yes,

issues should be resolved, but some relationships should be let go. As we grow and change, so do the people in our lives. As with my relationship with Sabrina, sometimes the changes mediate the break. "There may well be a time under heaven to close the door on friendships, especially the loose ties (Brestin, 1988: 117)."

Not all friendships work. Choosing friends is, for the most part, a guessing game. Often we want different things from our relationships than do the friends involved. If we are not willing to face this discrepancy, then we hurt each other unnecessarily. I have learned to say, "I'm not in a place where we can be close friends." While these words may wound, it is more truthful and faithful than to string someone along with no intentions of delivering a good relationship.

Some women constrict the life out of their friend, begrudging their other friendships. The same friend may be too needy to give. This is a cord that should be severed. Being a friend means befriending oneself, and when relationship with another stifles, harms or limits our lives, it is not a friendship but a vise.

There are several patterns of destructive relationships. Who cannot remember being used by someone who always takes but never gives. What of the emotionally abusive person who sees their role as one of making the friend feel inadequate, needy, guilty. Then there are women who are manipulative and use their knowledge of the friend as a weapon, such alliances must be ended if we are to move toward wholeness and health.

We may move on. We grieve for what we did not get out of a relationship. But we must learn also to celebrate what we did learn or receive. Friendships may be only for a season. It would be a shame not to reap the fruits of a passing season. In the words of the communion service of the Methodist church, "let these leave that others may come." There is often a cleaning out of the emotional closet and as sad as it may seem, this often includes the ending of friendships. It has been my experience that black women are **wont** to search for ways to keep friendships alive, even when they have been destructive. Somehow, we identify ourselves with the friend and must wonder what we are saying about ourselves when we say that someone we chose to love is no longer able to be in our lives.

We pastor one another, feeding each other's souls. This is strength for our journeys. We depend on each other, attending to each other, intending toward wholeness and contending for the best. We fight and cry and we reconcile. Sometimes we let go. We may hope for no better than this.

The vision of friendship as curing souls is basic. Spouses leave, children grow up, but while they may have different faces and names, friendship is constant. This is the nature of the God we serve. As black women we have made our way gingerly through the maze of time, we have seen our friendships as sacred, God-given and God-inspired. We are called to sanctify these sacred ties with our gifts and the offerings of ourselves. We call them holy by naming them. We model God in the midst of such relationships. We model human relationship with God, where we delight and rage, laugh and cry all in the name of <u>liking</u>. Yes, friends love each other with a fierce tenderness, but it is the sheer joy of being with another because they are good to be with that makes the friendship bond so powerful.

We minister to each as we soothe each other's wounds, prepare each other with our laughter and our love. We minister to each other as we speak the truth in love. We minister as friends when we allow others to enter our circle of friends. Such relationships deserve celebration and recognition. I began this piece with the recounting of my Sister-Friend party. I plan to be deliberate more often about telling the women who pastor me with their friendship how much I care for them.

Black women have articulated their need for one another well. Perhaps Toni Morrison (yr: 1990) said it best in *Song of Solomon*: "She needed what most colored girls needed: a chorus of mamas, grandmamas, aunts, cousins, sisters, neighbors, Sunday school teachers, best girl friends and what all to give her the strength life demanded of her -- and the humor with which to live it."

Endnotes

[1]Laura B. Randolph, *"Sisters of the Spirit: Networks Help Celebrites Deal with Fame and Pain,"* Ebony, July 1990, p. 38.

[2]Ibid.

[3]Ibid., p. 36

[4]Linda Tschirhart Sanford and Mary Ellen Donovan, *"Friends, Lovers and Spouses: The Power of Chosen Intimates," Women and Self-Esteem" Understanding and Improving the Way we Think and Feel About Ourselves,* (Harrisburg, Va.: R.R. Donnelley & Sons Co., 1985), p. 105.

[5]Lillian Rubin, *Just Friends: The Role of Friendship in our Lives* (New York: Harper & row, Publishers, 1985), p. 22.

[6]Sallie McFague, *Models of God* (Philadelphia: Fortress Press, 1987), p. 162.

[7]Lucille Clifton, *"For deLawd,"* In the Midst of Winter: Selections from the Literature of Mourning, Mary Jane Moffat, ed. (New York: Vintage Books, 1982), p. 156.

[8]Renita J. Weems, *Just a Sister Away: A womanist Vision of Women's Relationships in the Bible* (San Diego: Lura Media, 1988), p. 34.

[9]Judith Viorst, *Necessary Losses* (New York: simon & Schuster, 1986), p. 187.

[10]Mary Hunt, *Fierce Tenderness: A Feminist Theology of Friendship* (New York: Crossroads Publishing Co., 1991), p. 81.

[11]Eva Margolies, *The Best of Friends, the Worst of Enemies: Women's Hidden Power over Women* (Garden City, N.Y.: Doubleday & Company, Inc., 1985), p. 38.

[12]Tschirhart Sanford and Donovan, *Women & Self-Esteem*, p. 124.

[13]Rubin, *Just Friends*, p. 191.

[14]Kate Rushin, *"In Answer to the Question: Have you Ever Considered Suicide,"* The Black Women's Health book: Speaking for Ourselves, Evelyn C. White, ed. (Seattle: Seal Press, 1990), p. 3.

[15]Fague, *Models of God*, p. 160.

[16]Ibid., p. 268.

[17]Hunt, *Fierce Tenderness*, p. 38.

[18]Dee Brestin, *The friendships of Women: Harnessing the Power in our Heartwarming, Heartrending relationships* (Wheaton, IL: Victor Book, 1988), p. 36.

[19]Ibid., p. 35.

[20]Margolies, *Best of Friends*, p. 89.

[21]Marjory Zoet Bankson, *Seasons of Friendship: Naomi and Ruth as a Pattern* (San Diego: Lura Media, 1987), p.9.

[22]Ibid., p. xiv.

[23]Ibid., p. 45.

[24]Hunt, *Fierce Tenderness*, p. 117.

[25]Ibid., p. 81.

[26]Ibid., p. 151.

[27]Randolph, *"Networks,"* Ebony,. p. 38.

[28]McFague, *Models of God*, p. 162.

[29]Hunt, *Fierce Tenderness*, p. 39.

[30]Margolies, *Best of Friends*, p. 283.

[31]Viorst, *Necessary Losses*, p. 187.

[32]Tschirhart Sanford and Donovan, *Women & Self-Esteem*, p. 123.

[33]Ibid., p. 128.

[34]Hunt, *Fierce tenderness*, p. 102.

[35]Brestin, *The Friendships of Women*, p. 117.

[36]Toni Morrison, *Song of Solomon* (p. 190).

BIBLIOGRAPHY

Bankston, Marjory Zoet. *Seasons of Friendships: Naomi and Ruth as a Pattern*. San Diego: Lura Media, 1987.

Brestin, Dee. *The Friendships of Women: Harnessing the Power in our Heartwarming, Heartrending Relationships*. Wheaton, IL: Victor Books, 1988.

Clifton, Lucille, *"For deLawd." In the Midst of Winter: Selections from the Literature of Mourning*, Mary Jane Moffat, ed. New York: Vintage Books, 1982.

Hunt, Mary. *Fierce Tenderness: A Feminist Theology of Friendship*. New York: Crossroads Publishing Co., 1991.

McFague, Sallie. *Models of God*. Philadelphia: Fortress Press, 1987.

Margolies, Eva. *The Best of Friends, the Worst of Enemies: Women's Hidden Power over Women*. Garden City, N.Y.: Doubleday & Company, Inc., 1985.

Morrison, Toni. *Song of Solomon.*

Randolph, Laura B., *"Sisters of the Spirit: Networks Help Celebrities Deal with Fame and Pain."* Ebony, July 1990.

Rubin, Lillian. *Just Friends: The Role of Friendship in our Lives.* New York: Harper & Row, Publishers, 1985.

Rushin, Kate, *"In Answer to the Question: Have You Ever Considered Suicide."* The Black Women's Health Book, Evelyn C., White, ed. Seattle: Seal Press, 1990.

Sanford, Lina Tschirhart and Mary Ellen Donovan, *Women and Self-Esteem: Understanding and Improving the Way we Think and Feel About Ourselves.* Harrisburg, Va.: R.R. Donnelly & Sons Co., 1985.

Viorst, Judith. *Necessary Losses.* New York: Simon & Schuster, 1986.

Weems, Renita J. *Just a Sister Away: A Womanist Vision of Women's Relationships in the Bible.* San Diego: Lura Media, 1988.

When I am an Old Woman I Shall Wear Purple: An Anthology of Short Stories and Poetry, Sandra Martz, ed. Watsonville, Ca.: Papier-Mache Press, 1987.

Hollies, Linda H. *Inner Healing for Broken Vessels: Seven steps to Mending Childhood Wounds.* Joliet: Woman to Woman Publications, 1990.

Levin, Pamela. *Cycles of Power: A User's Guide to the Seven seasons of Life.* Deerfield Beach, Fl.: Health Communications, Inc., 1988.

Cooey, Paula M., et al., eds. *Embodied Love: Sensuality and Relationship as Feminist values.* San Francisco: Harper & Row, 1987.

Briscoe, Jill. *Thank You for Being a Friend: A Celebration of Friendship - Woman to Woman.* Grand Rapids: Zondervan Publishing House, 1980.

McGinnis, Alan Loy. *The Friendship Factor.* Minneapolis: Augsburg Publishing House, 1979.

Raymond, Janice. *A Passion for Friends: Toward a Philosophy of Female Affection.* Boston: Beacon Press, 1986.

Valerie J. Bridgeman Davis, M. Div., Austin
Presbyterian Theological Seminary, serves as one of
two clergy couples who co-pastor the Banah Full
Community Church in Austin, Texas. Ordained by
the Church of God, Anderson, Indiana, she has
served as writer for their Shining Light Survey, a
denominational magazine as well as writer for
Pathways To God, a church devotional and Sunday
school materials. Valerie is a much sought after
workshop and seminar leader who brings much to
enrich our lives with her poetry and reflective
writings. Presently, she works as Communications
Coordinator for Austin Metropolitan Ministries, an
Interfaith Group, and continues her clinical pastoral
education ties through her work at Seton Medical
Center in Austin. Married to Rev. Don Davis, she is
mother to Deon and Darus.

Driven Women

"Your mama raise a bunch of driven women."
Casually, he lifted the closed-off life in my well-kept
cedar chest.
He scurried into my past, picking up the really
hidden there.
Driven women, yes.
Mama was convinced -- and persuaded us, too --
you just can't trust a man, for nothing.
You have to do it all, on your own.
Desperation stalks when you believe you have to do
all
the taking care of yourself.
Mama was trying to save our souls -- at least our
lives.
We got a runaway fear down in our gut,
and have been running ever since.
"You all certainly overloaded on the helping
professions."
Matter-of-factly, she held up the locked-up spirit in
my dowry bag.
She sauntered in my memories, dusting off the truth
buried there.
Overloaded women, yes.
I started a slow descent into numbness.
"Let's not think about this," my Little Girl pleaded.
"It scares me."
It scares the Big Grown Up me, too.. So we didn't
think about it. Then. But a litany started forming in
my mind.

Mama was a bad somebody.
Teacher/seamstress/nurse/preacher/writer/
singer/seamstress/reporter/chaplain/pastor/
psychologist.
Who were we trying to convince?
What were we trying to "fix"?
"We need to give something back," she said.
To Whom? And somebody, please, tell me Why.
"Your mama raise a bunch of driven women."
She was driven, too, D.
Trying to settle it once for all that women make the
best drivers!
Mama just didn't know it would make us all
desperate.

Valerie J. Bridgeman Davis
November 25, 1991

CHAPTER 10

Mother and Daughter Issues:
Ties That Bind and Bless
Mary M. Wise

This chapter has been written because daughters are an extension of their mothers. As daughters, we sometimes struggle to live up to the high standards set by our mothers. In struggling, we sometimes fail to realize that maternal inheritance is filled with baggage from generation to generation. "By tracing these patterns through the generations, we could see the conscious and unconscious repetitions, correct for the best in our maternal inheritance, and get rid of the rest" (Friday, 1977:14). Yet, the reality is that as African-American women, we are locked into certain constrictive patterns. If we deviate from those patterns, we may then be classified as a rebellious child. There is a unique relationship which exists between mothers and daughters. African-American mothers and daughters are more unique, because the daughters emerge not only from their mother's womb, but also from their mother's "wounds" of intense struggle.

While interviewing a fifty year old woman, who is currently a daughter, mother and grandmother about "Mother and Daughter Issues" she said, "that which constricts, cuts off life. Freedom is needed to allow the child to make mistakes and to develop their own individuality. At the very least to allow that child to make decisions for themselves and accept the consequences for those decisions. Yet, allowing the child to grow, doesn't mean giving them total freedom. My daughter has certain weaknesses which I have contributed to, as a result of my inability to allow her enough freedom to make certain choices. I am now watching my daughter work to overcome those weaknesses. I wish it had been different." Ties that bind can leave scars for life unless we, as daughters and mothers, seek to achieve complete wholeness. This is accomplished when we come out of the closet and allow our souls to open up and experience the "Son" shine. It is time for liberation. It is time for reconciliation. The choice is up to the one who is hurting to find freedom. There is hope and that hope lies deep within our souls.

Professionally, over the past ten years, as an eclectic clinician and now as a pastor, I have found that every school of therapy has something to offer. To the wounded healers of the world and to those who are bound, this chapter will help you find strength within. Strength to change the negative ties that bind into ties that bless, as well as, strength to reclaim and celebrate the ties that bless (Phil. 4:10-14). Many times in our lives the pain overshadows the good and we fail to experience our blessings. Thus, we need to celebrate and praise God for all growth. Please note that some mothers or daughters may consciously make a choice to hold on to the ties that bind; while others will not be aware that they are bound. We need to remember at all times that we serve a God who will nurture, protect, and guide, if we will allow our Savior to be in control of our lives (Matthew 7:7). The following are some typical statements that in essence are negative ties that bind.

"You are just like your father. You have a nasty attitude. You're nothing like me".

"You are going to die and go to hell, if you don't change your ways".

"You should have listened to me in the beginning and you wouldn't be in this mess".

"Your kids aren't worth _ _ _ _".

"You very seldom find daughters now days who care for their mothers, like Carol cares for hers".

"I'll see you six feet in hell first".

"Why don't you get a husband, your kids need a father?"

"I can see why you're not married. If I were your husband, I'd beat your ass!"

"All that makeup makes you look like a whore".

"You are the cause of your childrens problems! YOU!"

What causes a mother to lash out at her daughter? What causes a mother to be so judgmental and accusative? In order for children to have a high opinion of themselves, which motivates them to strive for perfection, it is necessary for the mother (parents) to display affection, coupled with understanding and approval. When daughters feel rejected and criticize, they will being to feel worthless and project a "what's the use of trying attitude". Thus, "parents who feel relatively poor self-esteem are models whom children frequently emulate" (Schaefer & Millman in "How To Help Children With Common Problems").

Many African-American daughters are being forced to raise their children alone. Because, their men are finding it increasingly difficult to find jobs and keep them, coupled with increasing societal pressures and unresolved childhood issues, more and more African-American men are engulfed by drugs or in prison. Thus, many daughters are resigned to the fact that if they have to raise their children alone-they will. There are a select few, however, who have made a conscious choice to become pregnant and raise their child alone. This decision was reached because they did not desire to repeat the traumas their mothers experienced. What are those traumas their mothers experienced?

Susie, is 45 years old, divorced and a single-parent with three children. Her father exited her life when she was 2 years old and he died before she was 25 years old without having verbally communicated any feelings for his daughter. Susie was told he was an exceptionally brilliant man, though he did not possess the needed skills to be a father. He was a stern disciplinarian, who always said, "little children should be seen and not heard." Susie's mother, Mrs. K., was from a large family. She too was strict. She believed in "sparing not the rod to spoil the child" (Pro. 10:13, 13:24). As Susie reflected back over the years, she said, "I guess they had to be that strict if they wanted to stay in complete control." Susie shared the following portion of her story: There was never any privacy! Yet, we were taught to respect one another's things. We were taught to share, to love, to be there for each other and most of all to help others. She was taught that if you give a willing heart and make sacrifices then God would open up the windows of heaven and pour you out so many blessing you would not be able to receive them all. Society challenged those teachings and Susie began to have many doubts. Mrs. K's second marriage occurred during the time the bonds between fathers and daughters (ages 3-6) are being established, in a normal stage of development. It is also the time when little girls begin idealizing their fathers (see Dr. Bobbie McKay's book on The Unabridged Woman). Thus, Susie loved her stepfather very much and to her he was her real father. Then something happened to break down the family structure. Susie's stepfather became an abusive alcoholic. Her mother became a battered, overprotective, disciplinarian. When the abuse began, Susie's love for her mother out weighed everything and she sprang to her mother's defense. Only to be chased away by her stepfather with a belt. It was also during this time that Mrs. K. was hospitalized. Although, Susie couldn't remember the cause of the hospitalization, she could remember going to live with her aunt and grandmother for a long time. Then, the bomb was dropped! During Mrs. K.'s hospitalization, Susie's grandmother became ill and died.

She was unable to cope with death, because she had not gone completely through the grieving process. Susie and her mother's ties became strained when the baby sister entered the picture, when Susie became emotionally attached to her stepfather, and when her grandmother died.

The family structure began to fragment when abnormal traumas were added to the entire system. Thus, when Susie chronologically became an adult, she was still a child in the way she internalized her feelings for the opposite sex. She was constantly seeking to find a man who could live up to her fantasy. Through treatment, we were able to uncover that Susie repressed portions of her memory. The repression allowed her to face the fear of her mother leaving her like her grandmother did and never returning. It allowed her to face feelings of abandonment, loss, rejection, and worthlessness.

Being a mother is a unique experience. When our parents were born their parents did not have books to read or child development classes to attend, nor did most of us over the age of 35. So in reality, we learned as our parents did, through trial and error. In John Bradshaw's book, *Home Coming*, he talks about the wounded inner child growing into an adult, with a wounded inner child. The body has physically grown up but the emotional and psychological part of the person is still a child. If the child is wounded as in the following case of Kathy, she will live in a fantasy world in regards to her relationship with men.

Kathy had eleven brothers and sisters. The primary responsibility of raising them rested on their mother's shoulder's. It was Kathy's dream to have nine children when she married at the age of 21 years. Yet, she was determined not to be physically abused like her mother, so she married a man who did not drink or smoke. He was considered by modern standards, to be a good catch, a religious man with three years of college. Kathy and her husband set goals and talked constantly about their hopes and desires.

The first year of their marriage was truly an adjustment period, because Kathy's husband was totally different from her fantasy lover. Kathy had never experienced bonding with her father. Kathy's husband could not live up to her fantasies. She did not experience physical abuse like her mother, nevertheless, she was emotionally abused. This abuse was so devastating to her that she had finally admitted that she had made a mistake and left her husband after seven years. The loss she experienced caused her to go into seclusion for a year. The tie that bound their relationship was that she wanted to prove to her mother that not all men were bad and live up to her teachings, by remaining married for the rest of her life.

The blessing a mother shares with her daughter

220

comes when she empathizes with her. It comes when she shares the mistakes she has made. It comes when the mother can push her daughter out of the nest like a mother bird does and then say "Fly". "Fly" with all your might. You can do it! If the daughter fails, the mother is there to nurture the wounds and help her try again. Problems arise when the mother wants to live her life through her daughter. A mother can teach, preach, show by example, but eventually she has to allow the daughter to move out on her own.

As daughters push to break the cycle, by reading materials on child development and taking courses, they develop a better awareness of their own children's needs. Thus, they try to help their daughters positively go through the stages of development. Conflict arises when the mother downgrades the daughter's parenting skills and constantly questions her authority. Sometimes mothers fail to internally acknowledge that their daughters are now women and need to be treated as such.

Black mothers have been known to become annoyed when their grown daughters question their mother's authority. Jackie is a 33 year old woman with two children. Her mother came to live with her to help with the children while she was going to school. Jackie was studying to become a teacher. During Jackie's field education placement, she was able to observe the interaction, which takes place between "parent and child". Some of the mistakes she made as a single-parent became obvious. The relationship between Jackie and her mother became strained because she felt Jackie was too lenient. Jackie's mother refused to allow her to be the parent, unless there was something she didn't want to deal with. The children were caught between mother and daughter ties which were binding, conflicting, and constricting.

Jackie finally realized that she had to practice what she preached. "If you have an aught against your sister or your brother, go to them and tell them" (Matthew 5:23). Too many years of conflict over child rearing had passed before Jackie took the first step, to bring about resolution between her mother. Now she is ready to comfortably but firmly stand behind her own parenting skills. If a mother or daughter realistically know that they may never resolve the conflict between them, then they must find peace within themselves. Boundaries must be mentally set and then stuck too, because one cannot compromise their own integrity even for the sake of peace. Like the words of a poet, "to thine ownself be true". Standing up for your rights is not being disrespectful, if it is done out of love and with God's guidance. Through fasting, prayer and meditation, God will reveal how to gain inner peace. I cannot emphasize enough, never speak out in anger for what comes from the mouth truly comes from the heart. Many times in our lives, we need to know that we are okay, just the way we are! And we need to know that our mothers affirm us. If the mother is a wounded child, she is not capable of giving that affirmation in the way we may need. Thus, the daughter must find her worth within herself and quit waiting for Mom's approval. Daughters must begin to realize "I am somebody, because God didn't make junk"! Just as mothers need to realize that their identity is not dependent upon their daughters.

A woman's sexuality is one of the greatest gifts God created. The totality of our sexuality is not breasts, bottoms, legs or genitals. It is our total being. Many women born in the early 1900's believed that women were only put here to satisfy men and bring forth children. Scripturally that assessment is correct if your view is only a myopic one. God obviously had more in mind when we were created, otherwise we would not have erogenous zones or emotions. A woman's sexuality is wrapped up in her emotions, values, experiences and her whole body. As complex creatures, our sexuality does not begin in the womb. Each developmental stage of our life brings us from one point of awareness to another. Thus, our sexuality is more than the process of pregnancy, child bearing, menopause and aging.

Upon counseling with many mothers, I ask if they taught their daughters about their sexuality; the reply was always "yes". A mother's perception of all that their daughters "needed to know" was not the daughters perception of what she "needed to know". If a mother fails to teach her daughter about sex, the daughter will learn it from somewhere. The daughter will watch how the parents respond to each other and she will model that behavior. If the behavior is restricting and unemotional than that will be modeled.

The extent to which sexuality is discussed in

many churches is limited to fire and brimstone preaching against fornication or adultery. Some preachers are uncomfortable discussing ones sexuality. And because of this, it is viewed by some laity, that preachers must surely be asexual beings. When we take vows for the ordained ministry in the United Methodist Church we agree to "maintain the highest standards represented by the practice of fidelity in marriage and celibacy in singleness" (Judicial Council Decision 542, Discipline, 1988, par. 402.2, pg. 207). This by no means implies that our hormones are frozen in time or non-existent. Reality states we are all sexual beings, with needs, wants and desires. How we respond to our emotions is something different.

There are thousands of women who have been sexually abused as a result of either rape or incest. Diedra Kriewald wrote in "Hallelujah Anyhow", the results of a crisis survey on United Methodists. It stated that "one out of every thirty respondents had been raped and one in every nine had known of a family member or close friend who had been raped. The report concluded, however, that denial runs deep and we encountered disbelief and an amazing capacity to rationalize the findings. Denial is not usually productive. Christians must accept pain and name its cause honestly for themselves and before God (Kriewald, 1986: 103)." The most difficult step in the treatment process is admitting the violation to someone else. After admission, the pain must be released. "To let the pain go means that we no longer let suffering itself be the force that dominate our lives" (pg. 104). Removing the padlocks from the door of ones sexuality, requires that we must first be honest with ourselves. Second, face the problems and name it! Third, seek professional help. In order to forgive, the woman first confront her abuser. For me, the greatest reward in life is to know that someone is being healed.

Fourth, learn all you can about your sexuality. To this end, I would highly recommend Sheila Kitzenger's book, *Woman's Experience of Sex.*

Many books have been written over the past ten years showing people how to talk to another person without the person physically being present. This allows you the space to get in touch with your own feelings. Some have found journaling helps them to express their true emotions. Others do not like to write, so they use a tape recorder. I have found through practice that many clients who cannot physically confront the abuser, receive more success through what I call imaginations and response (See Exercise I).

EXERCISE I

Two straight back chairs are needed and should be positioned, facing one another. Once you are seated, face the other chair. Relax! Focus on relaxing every part of your body. After this is accomplished your eyes may be either opened or remain closed (I prefer closed eyes because it is easier to visualize the other person without distractions). Imagine the person who has hurt you sitting in the chair facing you. Allow yourself to feel their presence. Allow yourself to feel all of the emotions that are coming forth. Remembering at all times that they cannot hurt you again. But your feelings are still authentic. Now, tell them what's on your mind. Ask them whatever questions you have. When you are through, relax and breath deeply. Now, move into their chair. You are now them. Sit quietly and try to experience their feelings. Take as much time as you need. Allow them to answer the questions you posed. Allow them to speak through you and acknowledge their feelings and thoughts. Try to experience all of their emotions. When they are finished, breath deeply and relax. When you are ready, come back to the present reality. If you still have something to say or more questions, repeat the process till you are through. When you are completely satisfied, stop.

After doing the exercise, some daughters have found they have a deeper appreciation for their mother as a woman and as a friend. It is time to face the ghost which lurks within and name them. It is time to deal with our conscious and unconscious reality. Some have had to do this exercise several times in order to move forward to what we call wholeness. Others have found that they need someone to be a guide, as they go through the exercise. Thus, as we said in seminary, "we are becoming".

Ties that bind are not intentionally set up to hinder a mother and daughter relationship. As mentioned previously, daughters are an extension of their mothers. We attempt to model their positive behavior. If our self-esteem is not too fragmented we will work hard at not making the same mistakes our mothers did.

Sharon, a 51 year old grandmother and mother of 3 daughters was abandoned by her father while still in the womb. Sharon was raised by her twice divorced mother whom she loves very deeply. Although they remain in constant touch with one another, still, Sharon had never admitted to her mother the problems she had believing in herself. "The reality is that deep within, I'm scared. Mother's edicts were inflexible and I received them as such, which is why it disturbed me so much, that her preaching and teaching were often in direct contradiction to the ways she lived her life. Oh! I know the old adage, 'Don't do as I do-Do as I say', but for me that just doesn't wash".

It was at this point that I asked Sharon if she could recall for me any concrete examples of the mixed signals she received. She said, "One of my mother's cardinals rules was that male violence of any kind which was directed, toward females, was totally unacceptable and wouldn't be tolerated. The reality was that many times mother allowed her husband to physically abuse her and sometimes she even appeared to provoke the abuse. As I became an educated woman, I wondered, did she believe what she preached?"   Given the time frame in which Sharon was growing up, it is understandable why her mother taught her the things a woman needed to know, about raising a family and taking care of a home. Yet, Sharon needed more than her mother was capable of giving. "My mother taught me many positive things, such as, following orders, pleasing those in authority, that it was all right to be different, and that there are consequences for your actions.

Our society is full of double messages. Sharon projected a lot of hostility toward her mother. Thus, I felt compelled to suggest to her that she herself had been guilty of sending out mixed messages. Sharon took a major step in her life when she decided to change the cycle and question the teachings of her mother. The next step after acknowledging the problem was to do something about it. Sharon refused to experience the same kind of abuse as her mother. Yet, she allowed her husband to tear down her self-esteem. Still a gusty fighter, Sharon broke away from the constricting ties and began to rebuild.

As Black women we have a choice as to whether we are going to adhere to the messages, or allow ourselves to be confused by them, or fight for what we believe. Remember, Mother's and daughter's relationships will always be in constant motion. One moment everything is blessed and the next moment binding. Yet, binding as we have seen is not necessarily negative. These ties are a bond which nothing on this earth, can remove.

Thus, it is the quality of the relationship that holds you together when nothing on earth seems rational. Also, it is that special bond which causes a grown woman to travel miles back home to her mother, put her arms around her and give her a big hug. And then, lay down beside her for an hour or two and return to her own home, refreshed revived, and satiated. Refueling! Every child will return to their mother for fueling, no matter how old they are if that child bonded with their mother. I used the word child, because sons refuel too. However, the bond between a mother and a daughter appears to be stronger, because they are of the same gender and have many of the same tendencies.

In essence, daughters may try as hard as they might not to repeat the mistakes of their mothers, but the likelihood is they will. Thus, we need to constantly praise God for the undying strength our mothers possess. As, Renita J. Weems, *Just A Sister Away*, reminds us, "it takes a strong woman to leave what she knows -even if it is the love of a violent man - to face what she does not know, to face life alone" (pg. 83).

Many African-American mothers have had to face it alone and many more will have to in the future. As clinicians, pastors, psychotherapists, educators, laity, mothers and daughters, we need to be aware that many issues are hidden in the caverns of our souls. It is up to us as care providers to help the weak say I'm strong. It is up to us to provide space for healing. It is up to us to be aware that everyone has a story that needs to be told. Everyone has a song that needs to be sung. We can help those in need to tell their story and sing their song, if we are aware of the ties that bind and the ties that bless all mothers and daughters.

MOTHER/DAUGHTER

You have my eyes
You have my hair
You have my smile
None can compare.

You reach for hope
I only have pain
You ask for love
I am to blame.

Confused
Abused
Misused
Refused -

Becoming?
Like Me?
Lord, NO!
Restore, My Soul.

Womanistcare
Beyond Compare
Anointing with Oil
Through all the Toil!

Ties that Bind?
Wholeness!!

Mary M. Wise, 1991

P.S. To all those who disagree with my conclusions or find fault with my writing, don't blame or write to me. Please contact my mother.

BIBLIOGRAPHY

Anderson, Philip and Phoebe, *The House Church*, Abingdon Press: Nashville, 1975.

Barbach, Linnie Garfield, *For Yourself: The fulfillment of Female Sexuality*, Anchor Press: New York, 1976.

Becnel, Barbara Cottman, *The Co-Dependent Parent: Freeing Yourself By Freeing The Child*, Contemporary Books: Chicago, 1990.

Bradshaw, John, *HomeComing: Reclaiming and Championing Your Inner Child*, Bantam Books: New York, 1990.

Callahan, S.; Fenhagen, J.C.; Keith, J.N.; Mills, L.O.; Nelson, J. B.; and Southard, S., *The Pastor as Counselor*, The Pilgrim Press: New York: 1991.

Clinebell, Charlotte Holt, *Counseling for Liberation"*, Fortress Press: Philadelphia, 1976.

Clinebell, Howard J. Jr., *Basic Types of Pastoral Counseling*, Abingdon Press: New York, 1966.

Compton, Beulah Roberts & Galaway, Burt, *Social Work Processes*, The Dorsey Press: Homewood, Illinois, 1979.

Freud, Ann, *The Ego and The Mechanism of Defense*, International Universities Press, Inc.: New York, 1966.

Flax, Carol C. and Ubell, Earl, *Mother/Father/You: The Adult's Guide for Getting Along Great with Parents and In-laws*, Wyden Books: USA, 1980.

Friday, Nancy, *My Mother/My Self: The Daughter's Search for Identity:*, Delacorate Press: New York, 1977.

Gendlin, Eugene, *Focusing*, Bantam Books, Inc.: New York, 1981.

Hollies, Linda H., *Inner Healing for Broken vessels: Seven Steps to Mending Childhood Wounds*, Woman To Woman Ministries, Inc.: Joliet, Illinois, 1991.

Jewett, Claudia L., *Helping Children Cope with Separation and Loss*, The Harvard Common Press: Massachusetts, 1982.

Kriewald, Diedra, *Hallelujah Anyhow!: Suffering and the Christian Community of Faith*, The United Methodist Church: New York, 1986.

Kubler-Ross, Elisabeth, *On Death and Dying*, MacMillian Publishing Co.: New York, 1969.

Mahler, Margaret S., Pine, Fred, and BBergman, Anni, *The Psychological Birth of the Human Infant:*

Symboisis and Individuation, Basic Books, Inc.: New York, 1975.

Malone, Thomas Patrick and Malone, Patrick Thomas, *The Art of Intimacy*, Prentice Hall Press: New York, 1987.

McKay, Bobbie, *The Unabridged Woman: A Guide to growing Up Female*, The Pilgrim Press: New York, 1979.

McMillan, Terry, *Mama*, A Washington Square Press Publication: New YOrk, 1987.

Moltmann-Weddel, Elisabeth, *The Women Around Jesus*, Crossroad: New York, 1987.

Oates, Waynes E. & Oates, charles E., *People in Pain: Guidelines for Pastoral Care*, The Westminster Press: Philadelphia, 1985.

Petersen, J. Allan, *Conquering Family Stress: A Guide to Action in Times of Crisis*, Victor Books: Wheaton, Illinois, 1978.

Rapoport, Rhonda and Robert N., Strelitz, Ziona, *Fathers, Mothers & Society*, First Vintage Books: New York, 1980.

Schaefer, Charles E. & Millman, Howard L., *How To Help Children with Common Problems*, Van Nostrand Reinhold, New York, 1981.

Smith, Archie, Jr., *The Relational Self: Ethic & Therapy from a Black Church Perspective*, Abingdon Press: Nashville, 1982.

Weems, Renita J., *Just A Sister Away: A Womanist Vision of Women's Relationship in the Bible*, LuraMedia: San Diego, California, 1988.

Wise, Carroll A., *Pastoral Psychotherapy*, Jason Aronson: New York, 1973.

Mary M. Wise, ACSW, and M. Div., The Chicago
Theological Seminary is pastor of South Deering-
Pullman United Methodist Churches in Chicago,
Illinois. Mary has an extensive background in both
the clinical social work field and pastoral
experiences. Ordained in the Northern Illinois
Conference of the United Methodist Church, Mary
does preaching, teaching, workshops and seminars
which pull together the multi functions of ministering
to the whole person. A writer, poet, consultant,
Mary is mother to son, Daniel and daughter,
Carmieka.

Woman to Woman Ministries, Inc.
P.O. Box 0222, Joliet, IL 60434-0222

WOMANISTCARE:
HOW TO TEND THE SOULS OF WOMEN
Volume 1

_____ YES! Reserve me _____ copy(ies) of WOMANISTCARE. I am enclosing $14.99 (+2.00 postage/handling) for each book. (Total $16.99) make checks payable to WTMWI.

Name_____

Address_____

City _____ State _____ Zip _____

Phone ____(___)_____

MAIL ORDER TO: Woman to Woman Ministries, Inc.
                 P.O. Box 0222, Joliet, IL 60434-0222

Woman to Woman Ministries, Inc.
P.O. Box 0222, Joliet, IL 60434-0222

WOMANIST RUMBLINGS:

A PLACE TO RECORD YOUR STORY

_____ YES! Reserve me _____ copy(ies) of My 365 Day WOMANIST RUMBLINGS Journal. I am enclosing $19.95 (+4.00 postage/handling) for each journal. (Total $23.95) make checks payable to WTMWI.

Name _____

Address _____

City _____ State _____ Zip _____

Phone ___(___)_____

MAIL ORDER TO: Woman to Woman Ministries, Inc.
                 P.O. Box 0222, Joliet, IL 60434-0222

WOMANIST RUMBLINGS

Do you suffer from emotional scars from your childhood?

Are your relationships plagued with doubts and fears?

Do you dread success and growth?

If you answered "Yes",
it's time for this book!. . .

Rev. Linda H. Hollies, the dynamic founder and executive director of **Woman To Woman Ministries**, Inc., and pastor of Richards Street **United Methodist Church**, has written the *ultimate* book that shows you how to:

Soothe those childhood hurts
Be in touch with your *authentic self*
Become more successful in your family, relationships and career. . . *in 7 easy-to-follow steps!*

If you are ready for renewal and a *spiritual* re-direction towards wholeness and *abundant life*, you need more than outer healing **you need**

Inner Healing For Broken Vessels
Seven Steps To Mending Childhood Wounds
Published by Woman To Woman Ministries Inc. Publications

- -

Yes! I want **"Inner Healing"**! Enclosed is my donation of $10.00 (+2.00 postage/handling) for each book. (Total $12.00) make checks payable to WTWMI.

Name _____

Address _____

City _____ State _____ Zip _____

Phone __(___)_____

MAIL ORDER TO: Woman to Woman Ministries, Inc.
P.O. Box 0222, Joliet, IL 60434-0222

ISBN 1-880299-00-3